Elwood

ELWOOD

THE STORY OF A CATHOLIC WORLD WAR II HERO

SISTER LUCIA TREANOR, FSE

Our Sunday Visitor
Huntington, Indiana

Our Sunday Visitor Publishing Division
Our Sunday Visitor, Inc.
200 Noll Plaza
Huntington, IN 46750
1-800-348-2440

ISBN: 978-1-68192-586-8 (Inventory No. T2454)
eISBN: 978-1-68192-587-5
1. BIOGRAPHY & AUTOBIOGRAPHY—Military.
2. BIOGRAPHY & AUTOBIOGRAPHY—Religious.
3. RELIGION—Christianity—Catholic.
LCCN: 2021940234

Cover design: Tyler Ottinger
Cover art: Courtesy the Department of Defense POW/MIA Accounting Agency
Interior design: Lindsey Riesen

PRINTED IN THE UNITED STATES OF AMERICA

This book is dedicated to my mom, who loved her cousin Elwood, to Charlie Casey, in gratitude for his assistance with the early years, and to all families who have lost a serviceman or servicewoman in the defense of freedom.

I wish I could tell you about the South Pacific. The way it actually was. The endless ocean. The infinite specks of coral we called islands. Coconut palms nodding gracefully toward the ocean. Reefs upon which waves broke into spray, and inner lagoons, lovely beyond description.

— James A. Michener, *Tales of the South Pacific*

Contents

Foreword 9

Finding Captain Euart 13

1. Schoolboy Days 19

2. Bicycles and Truth 27

3. An NFL Championship Team 37

4. Falling in Love 45

5. The 1938 Hurricane..59

6. The Call of Uncle Sam 71

7. The *President Coolidge*...81

8. On the High Seas 91

9. Disaster Strikes..99

10. A Captain's Duty..105

11. The Aftermath.. 113

12. Notifications 121

13. Official Inquiries and Other Tragedies..129

14. Elwood Found... 135

15. In Memoriam.. 139

Bibliography 145

Notes 151

FOREWORD

After safely landing an Airbus A320 in New York City's Hudson
River on January 15, 2009, Captain Chesley Sullenberger, the US
Airways pilot in command of the plane, which had lost its engines
after hitting a flock of Canada geese, was called a hero by grateful
passengers and television commentators.

"No," he said. "A hero is someone who willingly puts his own life
in jeopardy for the good of others. We just did our job."

Captain Sullenberger's statement is both humble and profound.
Despite the enormity of the feat that he and his copilot performed,
they did not have to decide whether to risk their lives: the situation
was thrust upon them. What they demonstrated was not heroic virtue
but, rather, consummate skill.

The story of the sinking of the United States Army Transport
President Coolidge offers an opportunity to applaud both the skill of
Master Henry Nelson, who saved his troops, and the true heroism of
Capt. Elwood Euart, US Army, who risked his life for others. Of in-
terest to anyone who has contemplated the formation of what we call

character, the story presents the people and events that helped to build the kind of interior strength that great authors have often portrayed.

We encounter this sort of strength in the *Iliad*'s Hector but not in Achilles; in Galahad of the Arthurian legends but not in Lancelot; in Duke Vincentio of *Measure for Measure* but not in his deputy; in the king of Brobdingnag but not in Gulliver; in *David Copperfield*'s Mr. Peggotty but not in Steerforth; in *Sense and Sensibility*'s Elinor Dashwood but not in Marianne; in Billy Budd but not in Claggart; and in the priest in *A Farewell to Arms* but not in Lieutenant Henry.

The particular virtue that Captain Euart displayed was *fortitude,* which is mental and emotional strength in the face of danger. In a discussion of another virtue, faith, St. John Henry Newman — the nineteenth-century Anglican priest, poet, and theologian who later became a Roman Catholic cardinal — gives an insight that seems useful here. In Sermon 10, he distinguishes faith from reason, pointing out that the former "does not demand evidence so strong as is necessary for what is commonly considered a rational conviction"; rather, "it is mainly swayed by antecedent considerations." He observes that "the mind that believes is acted upon by its own hopes, fears and existing opinions." This also seems to be true of the virtue of fortitude.

Absent previous moral struggles that have been reflected upon and overcome, it is difficult, perhaps even impossible, for a moment of danger, fear, or temptation to be met by virtue. That opportunity may slide by, or worse, overwhelm, even a good person.

What are these "antecedent considerations" then? Newman suggests "hopes, fears, and existing opinions." The hero of our story experienced all three in radical situations that must have seemed unfair and terribly challenging at the time. He may not have met them with perfect grace, but it is clear that he learned from them, or he would not have been able to give the gift of himself so purposefully as to reveal an excess, a superabundance, of love for his men.

I have tried to shine a spotlight on a few of the events in his early life that would have tested his mettle and to introduce the family, friends, and soldiers who accompanied him on what is ultimately a spiritual journey.

* * *

Like many members of my family, I first learned Elwood's story when I was eight or nine years old. Born three months before he died, I am the daughter of his first cousin Lucy (Casey) McCaffrey. His sister Monica was my godmother, and his sister Eleanor later became my brother Tom's good friend. I remember Mom explaining to me that Elwood had been "lost at sea" in the South Pacific.

"How did he die, Mom?" I asked.

"Not by enemy fire."

"What do you mean?"

"He was killed by our own American mines, friendly mines, explosives set in the sea to blow up the Japanese." Mystified, I persisted.

"But how could that have happened?"

"It shouldn't have happened," she said grimly, and I can still feel the sorrow in her words. The death of a soldier, every soldier, is a family tragedy; but it is especially poignant when it happens by our own hand.

The story, as I have told it, is a dramatized biography. I have gathered as much information about Elwood as I could from relatives and friends, added research into the times and places where he lived, which I have documented in the endnotes and in the bibliography, and, failing a fact or two, dramatized what I believe would have been the event and persons involved. I found myself on my own only with the death of Adeline Belliotti, as my source was unclear about the details of the romantic rupture.

I am particularly indebted to three members of my family who remembered Elwood, two of whom have now died: his cousins Charles and Edward Casey and Roselyn Smith McCoy; to my sister, Maryann (McCaffrey) Knag, who helped with interviewing; to Paul Vallee, keeper of the memories; and to Walt Buteau for his fine reporting.

For details on the South Pacific, Peter Stone's book *The Lady and the President* was invaluable, as was Tim Richie's tracking down Rex Moli on Espiritu Santo for an interview.

I would also like to thank James Dodson for his essay on the

1938 hurricane; Matthew Laird Acred for his *Asisbiz* blog; Major K. Graham Fuschak for his master's degree thesis on the 43rd Infantry Division; John Hogrogian for National Football League history; Leah Nahmias for her paper on the Providence Cycledrome; Paul S. LoVerde, bishop emeritus of the Diocese of Arlington, Virginia; Karen Luchetti; and the many Rhode Island reporters who covered Elwood's military funeral.

Finally, thank you to my community, the Franciscan Sisters of the Eucharist, who have afforded me the time to write this account of heroic virtue and have encouraged me with affection and support; and to my family — Euarts, Caseys, McCaffreys, and Treanors — whom I love.

Sister Lucia Treanor, FSE
Franciscan Life Process Center
June 2, 2021

FINDING CAPTAIN EUART

Rex Moli was not at all nervous about diving into the world's most famous shipwreck that day. As an employee of Santo Dive Tours, he had logged countless underwater hours on the *President Coolidge* in his sixteen years diving off the New Hebrides island of Espiritu Santo in Vanuatu. He knew the World War II ship's story well: how she had hit two friendly mines in the Segond Channel, how her captain had purposely grounded her on the reef, and how almost all of the five thousand soldiers had climbed down to safety before she sank. Everyone on Espiritu Santo — in fact, most everyone in the South Pacific — knew the story of the *Coolidge*.

But this day in mid-June 2012, Rex was diving alone because he loved her, not the way he loved his wife and children, but the way Melanesian highlanders love their seductive cup of *kava*. It relaxed him to glide through the azure waters, gently moving his flippers like a shadow-finned soldierfish. As he descended into the deep, a couple of eels crossed his path, then a curious grouper, four angels, and some pennant fish. The prow of the *Coolidge* gradually revealed itself ahead of him in the shape of a try square, and, as always, he thought of the American who had gone down with the ship. A visiting veteran had said that the man had been a carpenter before the war.

Maybe today will be the day, Rex thought, swimming along the starboard side above a row of crusty portholes. A three-inch gun loomed in the blue shadows, a mark of the ship's wartime responsibility. Then, as he floated over the promenade deck and down to C deck, the gigantic hull of the one-time luxury liner came into view in all her majesty. Rex loved this view as it melted away into the inky darkness.

* * *

Rex's day had begun quietly at home, not far from the Sarakata River. He had gotten up early to feed and water the chickens in the backyard under the tamanu tree, and he had thought that later he would spend time in the garden, working the taro and island cabbage. But first he wanted to check into the dive shop to see whether he would be needed.

Rex was one of ten divers whom Allan Power, owner of Santo Dive Tours, had on his roster. Some of them, like him, were ni-Vanuatu, natives of the island, who had been diving most of their lives. Often, the first one to arrive at work got to go with the eight o'clock group. Rex liked people, and he relished the morning dive because of the way the sun slanted on the water — and because good tips often rewarded a well-guided experience.

He walked with purpose that morning, but as he approached the shop, he saw the tour bus pulling out, dragging a cart full of equipment.

Too bad, he thought, entering the open, white, well-supplied building. He was met by Tim Richie, a master diver.

"*Yan wea?*" he asked in Bislama, the pidgin English of the islands. "Where is Yan?"

"Not here, Rex. He just left with Allan. Did you see him?"

"I was hoping to dive with them."

"Well, you can come with me to see whether they need another, if you like. I'm going out in a few minutes."

"*Tuff tumas!* Very awesome!"

Rex straightened up the tanks and goggles and put things in order as Tim checked the day's schedule. In a few minutes, they were on their way.

By the time they got to the wreck, however, the diving group had gotten smaller because several tentative novices had elected to stay in the coral garden for a while and dive later in the afternoon. Only Tim and Yan were needed. And so Rex found himself gliding alone down to C deck on that June morning.

Deep diving is a blessed experience for those lucky enough to have the strength and ability to do it. In its meditative silence, the hidden, watery world speaks paradoxically of the fecundity of nature and its singularity, of ecological complexity and cosmic simplicity. Rex liked to ponder the variety of creation that he saw — the fish and the waving plants — as a sign of the Creator.

This day, the water was quiet and calm as he slipped into Cargo Hold 2, floating inside and along the interior of the port side. He passed over some Army Jeeps tossed about, their tires layered with peach-colored scale, and near a bulwark he swam by a truck. He was looking for the American captain, knowing that he had to be there somewhere, even though it had been seventy years since the ship went down. He had scouted the area many times, but never found a trace of the young man. *This time*, he thought, *will be different.*

Passing the stewards' cabin on his way to the lobby, he glided into the crew's bathroom, a place he had rarely visited. Perhaps today he would disturb the silt that filled the room. He moved to the wall and began digging gingerly, pushing aside the accumulated watery soil slowly and gently, aware that too much movement would make vision impossible. There was nothing in the corner, so he moved a couple of feet to the left and began again. His slow-motion nudges were careful, requiring the patience of a man skilled in underwater investigation. Like all the divers, he had been taught by Allan Power how to travel through the ship by degrees, treating her lightly, deliberately, and with consideration for her seemingly timeless beauty and mystery.

Then his hand hit something hard and loose. *Did it move?* There was a smoothness under his fingers; he was sure of it. He extended his thumb to explore the shape, and whatever it was slid several inches sideways. Finally, he grasped at it, and gradually brought it up for a look: it was a bone. Reaching down again, he felt others: they were human bones. *Yes,* he thought. *I have found him. I have found Captain Euart!*

The young captain's presence had been palpable to the ni-Vanuatuans of Espiritu Santo for years, and especially to the professional divers who knew they probably had skirted him many times. In a way, he was the spirit of the ship. Even the ordinary residents of the island knew him since, soon after the sinking, there had been memorial services at a nearby white stone marker that read:

In Memory of
Captain Elwood J Euart
103 Field Artillery Battalion
USA
October 26, 1942

An American flag and a Vanuatuan flag fluttered behind the marker. Rex knew that there would be a service later in the fall, as there had been on other anniversaries. At six in the morning, MC Kevin Green would begin the service under an archway of orchids by reminding everyone that "the kingdom of heaven is theirs," and Father Luke, vested in red and white, would pray: "Eternal God and Father, whose love is stronger than death, we rejoice that the dead as well as the living are in thy love and care, and are remembered." The Vanuatu Mobile Force (VMF) Santo, standing smartly at attention in their moss-green and red uniforms, would watch as Sanma Province SG Joel Path laid a pink hibiscus wreath at the marker and Luganville Municipal Council's Peter Sakita placed a leafy one there on behalf of the mayor. After the VMF commander, Capt. Benjamin Barney, led a moment of quiet prayer, clear trumpet notes would break the silence, and those in attendance would walk to the shore to place flowers on the water. Then there would be refreshments from Coral Quays. It would be a fitting October memorial seventy years after the tragedy. Rex thought, *This year will be different.*

Upon finding the bones, he knew that they were the captain's remains, and that they belonged not to him, but to the young man's country and to his people. He resolved to treat them with reverence, first gathering them together and then secreting them in a safe place. He swam quickly through the ship and up to the surface, telling the news to his colleague in whispered tones.

"I have found him, Yan."

"Yes?"

"Yes, in C deck."

"We had better tell Allan."

Back at the dive shop, they found Allan Power.

"I found something just now, Allan."

"Did you now, Rex? Was it on the ship?"

"Yes, on C deck. I had come in from the prow and then Cargo 2."

"What did you find?"

"I found bones, human bones. It's Captain Euart, Allan."

"Oh, my stars! Do you think so?"

"Yes, I do."

"Are you sure? It might be just animal bones, you know." He sounded skeptical. "This is what I want you to do."

"No, it's not an animal."

"This is what you do. You dive again in the afternoon and bring up one of the bones for me to check to make sure that it *is* a person."

"That's good. I will do it."

In the afternoon, Rex and Yan returned to the ship to retrieve one of the bones that lay deep within the sediment. Rex took it to Allan, who, recognizing the truth of the find, phoned the American authorities. Afterward, Rex returned it to the place where he had found the others. Only then did he discover the notched, gilded-metal oblong that set him at ease. It had been partly blackened with age but still lay among the bones, attached to a brown leather tie with a black hasp. The words read:

ELWOOD J EUART
0-374388 T42   0
MRS E F A EUART
444 POWER RD
PAWTUCKET R I   C

Rex was grateful for confirmation that he had found the American captain, and he thought about the young soldier. How old was he? Did he have a family? Where in America was this place "Pawtucket" with the strange-sounding name?

1

SCHOOLBOY DAYS

Pawtucket is a city in the smallest state with the longest name: Rhode Island and Providence Plantations, respectively, as every schoolchild in "Little Rhody" learns. In the language of its first settlers, the Narragansett Indian Tribe of Rhode Island, *pawtucket* means "the meeting of the waters": the fresh-water falls of the Blackstone River coming down from Worcester, Massachusetts, and the brackish tidal waters of the Seekonk River coming up from the Atlantic Ocean. The city, founded in 1671, was the site of America's first cotton mill, built a hundred years later by Samuel Slater. Pawtucket has been a center of industry ever since, its falls providing power for gristmills, sawmills, and iron forges.

By the early twentieth century, Pawtucket was predominantly populated by first- and second-generation English, French Canadians, Irish, and Italians. Elwood's parents, Elwood Francis Aloysius and Winifred (Casey) Euart, who were of Celtic roots, moved their large brood to a comfortable, middle-class home on Power Road near the Providence-Pawtucket city line in 1923. Theirs was a faithful, Catholic family.

Born on January 28, 1914, the first year of the Great War, Elwood Joseph was the second of seven children: Rita, Elwood, Mary Monica, John, Eleanor, Leonard, and Ruth. His father was a self-taught teacher and guidance counselor at Samuel Slater Junior High School in the public school system that the children attended. His mother, Winnie, described by her relatives as a woman with a "beautiful personality," superintended their busy home and the special needs of her youngest. The Euarts lived not far from North Main Street, a major thoroughfare leading from the domed capitol in Providence to the central district of Pawtucket. In Elwood's youth, everything happened on or near North Main: the silver crafting of the Gorham Manufacturing Company, shopping, the circus, hockey games at the arena, bicycle races and Steam Roller games at the Cycledrome, and Rhode Island National Guard drills at the Armory of Mounted Commands.

Elwood's school years were the interbellum years, when the state of Rhode Island, having passed through its slave-trading period and survived Lincoln Steffens's charge of "a state for sale," had accepted an influx of immigrants and transitioned from Republican to Democratic control in state government. The people of the city of Pawtucket were struggling with the decline of its textile industry, the rise of organized labor, the rapid construction of churches, and tension between ethnic groups. During this period, several public elementary schools were constructed to serve a growing population. Teachers, often managing overcrowded classrooms — there were a thousand students in Samuel Slater Junior High when it opened in 1925 — knew that they had to maintain order.

Elwood had such a teacher in the fourth grade. She taught everything: reading, spelling, numbers, drawing, nature study, and gardening. One day, when she was writing on the blackboard, she caught Elwood passing a note — or so she thought.

"Elwood Euart, I saw that. Stand up." She regularly watched what was happening in the class when her back was turned by checking the reflection in the picture of President Coolidge that was just slightly tipped above the poster of the cursive alphabet. This time, however, Elwood's seat was partially obstructed, and he was wrongly accused, but he stood up anyway.

"Miss Boynton, I didn't pass the note," he insisted.

"Elwood, you did. Now go sit down in the back bench."

"But honest, I didn't."

"Just go to the bench, or I will send you out into the hall," she ordered, raising her voice. When he protested his innocence again, Elwood ended up sitting in the hall for the rest of the morning. Later that day, he unhappily complained to his mother.

"Miss Boynton blamed me for passing a note during numbers, but I didn't," he whined, expecting pity from a mom who doted on her eldest son.

"Buddy, if you didn't do it this time," she observed, "you did it before. She's just catching up." Winnie, married to and very much in love with a teacher, would always support her children's teachers.

Besides his sisters and brothers, Elwood had friends on his block. After school and scouting, they played baseball in the street or in an undeveloped part of St. Francis Cemetery. In the fall, they played football without helmets or pads. What had been a college game was beginning to take off professionally, although not yet rivaling in number of fans the teams that regularly filled Boston's Fenway Park for baseball. There were, however, local football clubs all over New England with names such as the New Britain Hardware, the New London Submarine Base, the New Haven Blues, and the Bridgeport American Chain. Providence boasted a semi-pro team called the Steam Roller that played nearby, and it did well enough against the club teams to be invited to join the National Football League in 1925 for a fee of one hundred dollars.

At twelve years old, when he entered Samuel Slater, Elwood had a ruddy complexion, brown hair, and a perpetual smile. Of average build, he was beginning to pay attention to the Steam Roller.

"Hey," he said one day to his friend George Costa. "My Aunt

Anna told me a great joke."

"Yeah?"

"Did you hear about the football player's wife, who opened her door to the policeman?"

"Nope," replied George. "What happened?"

"The policeman had a sad look on his face. 'Ma'am,' he said. 'Your husband just got run over by a steamroller.'

" 'Oh, dear,' she answered looking down. 'Just slip him under the door.' "

The joke made the rounds of the school, even though the press wasn't giving much space to Steam Roller games yet.

Once in the National Football League, the Steam Roller began to play against established teams such as the Frankford Yellow Jackets, the Detroit Wolverines, the New York Giants, and the Green Bay Packers. One game that *was* hyped by the papers in the Steam Roller's seven-year NFL run was the first pro football game ever played in Boston. It happened in 1925 against the Chicago Bears, with well-known halfback Red Grange, called "the Galloping Ghost," who had signed with Chicago and was on a whirlwind post-college trip. His opponents on the Providence team included Jim Crowley and Don Miller, formerly of Notre Dame's Four Horsemen, and four Brown University alumni, including an early black player, Fritz Pollard. The Steam Roller won the game, 9–6. An account reported by the Associated Press assessed the Galloping Ghost's performance: "Grange appeared tired and listless, and when he retired from the game, after playing exactly forty-four minutes, he was booed by a few hundred of the spectators. The now wealthy Wheaton iceman played safety-first football during his stay of the game."[1]

Back in Providence, the fans were jubilant, and Elwood's family watched with interest as a strong Steam Roller team held its own in the middle of the NFL pack for the next couple of years. Then, in 1928, it burst forth as the best football team in the nation — but that is getting ahead of our story. The young boys of Power Road, who wrestled with a pudgy football that was not so streamlined as the ones used today, were learning a new national sport.

In the hot summer months, the same bunch, including Elwood's sister Mary Monica, would try to thumb a ride up Cobble Hill Road to Stump Hill Reservoir in Saylesville for swimming. The pond had been providing drinking water to the area since the nineteenth century, so it was a trick to get in without being seen. The kids wore bathing suits under their clothes, and someone always had to play lookout, which minimized the fun a bit. Their tricks worked for a while, until Winnie told Elwood that it was not okay to swim in the drinking water.

For Elwood and Monica, as she later preferred to be called, the real treat was a family weekend at Slacks Pond on the outskirts of Greenville. There, two of his uncles — Ed, who was a contractor, and Tom, a carpenter — were building a respite from the city heat at the top of a hill. All the children liked to splash and have their dad dunk their heads at the water's edge, and the bigger ones would swim a ways out. Elwood enjoyed that too, but even more he liked helping with the carpentry. Perhaps he had a sense that the hard work was manly; and besides, he savored the smell of his uncle Tom's cigar.

In August 1926, Elwood's uncles were working on the outside walls and roof of the rustic summer cottage. They had completed a large, open combination kitchen, dining, and sitting area with a fireplace in the center and had framed the back bedroom. A great front porch that would overlook the water from between the white birches and tall oaks was in the works.

One hot afternoon, when the cicadas were singing and the moss under his bare feet felt refreshingly cool, Elwood asked his uncle Tom whether he could build something. He had been helping for quite some time, bringing tools and water to his uncles, and he began to think that he could contribute to the family project. He wanted to make shelves for his aunt's dishes — the same aunt who had told him the joke about the steamroller. Uncle Tom, who worked for McDuff Coal and Lumber, knew that boys Elwood's age came with their dads looking for saws at the shop and thought that making the shelves would be a good experience for Elwood. He helped Elwood pick out the right size wood and showed him how to handle the carpenter's essential tools.

The two of them set up a work area with sawhorses in a gravel space at the top of a flight of steps that descended steeply to the water. The uneven stairs were made of tree logs to hold in the soil and had a railing made of the trunks of small trees. At the bottom was a pump set in a round cement base over a well and a long-handled, white enamel farmhouse cup with a blue line on the lip. The whole family used it. From his perch at the top of the stairs, Elwood could see everything that was going on below him: the little cousins Charlie and Ted running around looking for acorns and puffball spores, his sister Monica and cousin Lucy swimming by the boathouse, and his Aunt Anna chatting with his mom near the water.

He and Uncle Tom set to work. First, they measured the places to cut and then marked them with a pencil. Elwood set the wood on the sawhorses and began pushing the saw back and forth. In the beginning, it went well. He had decided to work on the back of the unit first, because the wood for it was thin; but when he got to the shelves, the effort started to test his muscles, the day seemed to grow hotter, and the sawdust tickled his nose and stuck to his skin. It didn't seem so much fun anymore, especially since, by then, all the others were frolicking in the cool water below him.

"How are ya doin'?" inquired Uncle Tom, coming around the corner of the house. He complimented Elwood on the rectangular piece that was finished and noticed that the boy was struggling to cut through the end of the shelf.

"Having trouble?" he asked.

"It's hard to get through this wood," Elwood grumbled. "My arm is tired."

"That's because the wood's thicker. Want a tip? When you start a job — any job, whether it is work or study — always try to figure out what part is the hardest and do it first. You are the freshest and strongest at the beginning and will be able to do it well. Then, when you are getting tired, do the easiest part, or the part you like the best, because it will not seem as hard."

"So I should have noticed that the shelves were thicker and cut them first, and then taken on the backing."

"Exactly. Now let's see how fast we can get the rest of these done."
Uncle Tom's solid advice stood Elwood in good stead for many
years.

After finishing the shelves, it was time to wash off the grime from
the work. So Elwood ran down the hill and leaped into the pond, sailing a few feet over the shallows and plunging down to the brown,
leafy bottom. He swam over to where Monica and Lucy, who were
just two years younger, were unhitching the rowboat from its moor-
ing ring on the dock next to the boathouse. They had permission to
take the boat out to gather the wild blueberries that grew all along the
waterfront. Elwood got into the boat and rowed gently while the girls
put the berries in a yellow Autocrat coffee can saved for the purpose.
He could hear the pinging sound as they went in.

"They're going to taste good, Monica," he joked, looking at the
yellow and red label with the chirping bird. "A swallow will tell you."

"Funny guy, Buddy," she retorted with sarcasm. Lucy giggled. She
had heard the commercial on the radio.

They worked their way along the margin, selecting the dark-blue
berries — not the whites or the reds — to where the bushes hung
far out over the water. Above their heads, dragonflies teased the air,
and below, water bugs hopped into their own reflections in the boat's
shadow. It was restful work, and when they had a full can, Monica
dangled her feet over the back of the boat. They floated out into the
center of the pond to dally a bit, while Elwood explained his carpentry
project.

When the sun began to slant across the water, turning everything
to gold, even the cut window glass that was resting by the side of the
house, they knew it was time to be getting back for supper. Elwood applied himself to the oars, while Monica continued to drag her feet off
the stern. As they got to the boathouse, and she jumped up onto the
dock, she yelled in disgust: a bloodsucker was attached to her ankle.
It was dark and fat and had clearly gorged itself for an hour or more.

"Don't touch it, or it will break off in you," warned Elwood as he
hastened to secure the rowboat. "We need to get a match." He had
come by this information in his nature book, so he directed Lucy to

sit Monica on the seat in the boathouse, while he went to get matches from his uncle.

In a couple of minutes, there was a crowd hovering over Monica, watching Elwood apply a lighted match to the tail end of the leech. Immediately it withdrew its teeth from her skin and fell off, and their dad stamped on it. Uncle Tom, who had supplied the matches, pressed a clean hankie to the bloody wound, and everyone hurried up the stairs to find some cleansing alcohol. Monica's dad carried her inside, and in a few minutes, "Nurse Winnie" had drenched the spot with whiskey and applied a bandage. For a long time, Monica had a small scar just above her ankle bone to remind her of the day.

Since the cottage was not yet ready for occupancy, supper was a picnic. Elwood's mom and aunt Anna had packed fried chicken, potato salad, and greens, and they all sat under the trees to eat while the men drank Narragansett beer. The wild blueberries with cream, however, turned out to be the hit of the evening. Everyone ate until they were full, and when it began to get dark, they piled into the Euarts' and Caseys' Fords for the drive home.

These were happy summer weekends, and the opportunity to do carpentry and to swim hardened Elwood's muscles, beginning the development of a skill and a sport. By the time he was in high school, he was able to swim across the pond, a feat only the strongest swimmers could accomplish.

2

BICYCLES AND TRUTH

If the Ford was the means of transportation for the elders of the family, it was the bicycle that had captured the attention of the junior-high set. On one day in particular, Elwood learned a worthwhile lesson that involved bicycles.

It was late October 1927, and the neighbors were raking leaves when Elwood opened his door and found his friend George there, grinning.

"What's up, Big G?" he said as he regarded the short, scrawny ninth grader he had grown up with on Power Road.

"Not much," mumbled George, fumbling with the horn on his bike. "You doin' anything?"

"Not much," repeated Elwood.

"Wanna check out the 'Drome? Maybe we can see some Mead Rangers."

Elwood looked quizzically at his friend. They both knew that they were not supposed to hang around the Cycledrome, which was two miles away, because there had been fights at some of the races, with people drinking, making bets, screaming, and tossing slurs such as "wop" and "mick" at each other. Elwood's dad had told him it was "a man's place" and sometimes dangerous. He said women and boys didn't go there.

But George and Elwood were mad about bikes. They and their school friend Dominic had been following the Providence cyclist Vincent "Poosha" Madonna, a professional motor-paced racer, who had been winning everywhere. He had beaten the American champion George Chapman at New York's Velodrome, set the world speed record of sixty-seven miles per hour in Philadelphia, and made a thousand dollars for one night's racing. The boys often talked about the bikes the wheelmen rode in this risky sport. There was a rumor that Madonna had just bought a Boogmans Stayer. Their own Columbia bicycles from Sears and Roebuck faded in comparison.

Elwood wrestled with his conscience for a moment, but then shot George a thumbs up and, in a flash, grabbed his bike from the garage, kicked up the stand, and jumped on.

"Come on, Big G!" he shouted. "See who gets there first." Before the two knew it, they were picking up speed, and in the blink of an eye, they had crossed the Moshassuck River, taking the back way through Collyer and down Ann Mary to the steeply banked racing track. They could hear the buzzing of the motorized pacers even before they got there.

When it opened in 1925, the Providence Cycledrome was the largest bike course in the nation. It could seat thirteen thousand fans and had a five-lap track that was a little longer than a quarter of a mile, so that racers had to go 150 times around for a thirty-mile race. Every Tuesday and Friday night, touring professionals such as Poosha Madonna competed under the lights against talented locals before hundreds — sometimes thousands — of fans.

This Saturday morning, the boys were hoping to sneak in to watch the anklers practicing. Maybe they would get to talk to Madonna, if he were home; if not, maybe Frank DiPaolo, another favorite. He regularly beat all the home-grown talent — except, of course, Madonna.

They parked their bikes against the back of the 'Drome in the shadow of the wooden bleachers, slid through the end of the fence, and worked their way past the food stand to the ramp. Six racers were working out.

"I don't see Poosha," said Elwood.

"Me neither. And I don't see DiPaolo. Maybe they haven't come yet." At that moment, they were interrupted by Mr. Coppen, whom they knew as the manager of the Cycledrome.

"What are you boys up to?" he barked in a gruff voice. "You know you can't come in here unless you pay thirty-five cents."

"We only want to see the practice," explained Elwood.

"All the same, you're not supposed to be inside the gate."

"Okay. We're going," George said immediately. And the two of them sidled off in the direction of the food stand, which was just beginning to prepare for the arrival of the football players for a practice in the grassy oval center of the 'Drome.

"Do you think he will keep watching us, El?"

"No. We can get back in in a few minutes, when he goes to put the practice fees in his office," said Elwood, betraying at least one previous adventure. Just then, Elwood spied Frank DiPaolo coming in, and both boys ran toward him. The whole city of Providence was rooting for DiPaolo — not just the Italians, who had always supported Madonna — and his successes were often reported in the papers.

"Mr. DiPaolo, are you going to race on Tuesday?" called out George, who was more of a DiPaolo than a Madonna fan.

"I hope so, son. Are you going to cheer me on?"

"From the fence. I don't have thirty-five cents, but my dad might. He saw you last week."

"Oh, no. Then he saw the accident."

"He did. He said you wiped out on the track real bad."

"Take a look. Bloodied arm. I'll probably have scars. Pretty poor race that was."

"And you're still going to race?"

"Bet your life I am! The winner's pay is better than Bob Cremins gets in a month of pitching for the Red Sox! You bet I am!"

"Well, good luck, Mr. DiPaolo."

"Thanks, boys. Here, buy yourselves a cone," he offered, tossing them a dime. This kind gesture was pure heaven to a pair of young boys who idolized Frank and dreamed of racing bikes and speed records. Even more than the ice cream, they were already imagining the look on Dominic's face when they reported this turn of events.

So they headed over to the stand humming "I Scream, You Scream," a popular song by Fred Waring's Pennsylvanians. They bought a pair of maple-walnut cones, which they enjoyed as they peered through the stands, watching Frank work out on his Mead Ranger. The motor pacers were speeding around the track, and Frank looked good despite his recent fall. He had been fortunate in avoiding serious injury.

The sport of motor-paced cycling was dangerous. The cyclist pedaled his bike behind a leather-clad pacer who stood up on a motorcycle to lessen the wind resistance for the cyclist. This allowed the cyclist to benefit from the slipstream created, so he tried to pedal as near as possible to the motorcycle, which had a small roller attached to the back of it to prevent crashes if the cyclist got too close. The pacer controlled the speed of the race, and when the cyclist wished to pass another racer, he gave a signal. Then the pacer sped up to as much as sixty miles per hour, with the cyclist pedaling to stay connected. If the cyclist drifted out of the slipstream behind his pacer, he would slow down rapidly. If he lost his pacer, he was out of the race. There were frequent accidents when the racer got too close or when the tires burst at speed, and, because the racers did not wear helmets and the stands were close, accidents were sometimes fatal for both racers and fans. A crash in Berlin had killed nine when a motorcycle went into the stands and exploded.

"How hard do you think it is to ride like that without getting hurt?" mused Elwood.

"Those bikes are light. Probably it's mostly balance. If you keep your balance and are careful, nothing will happen," said an optimistic

George.

"It looks exciting to me."

"Uh-huh. It is, I think."

"Look at Frank. He makes it look easy." At this point, Mr. Coppen crossed the track from the oval on the way to get things ready for the Steam Roller players, then disappeared into his office behind the stands, so the boys eased back down to the ramp to get a better look at the bikes and the pacers. It wasn't long before Frank waved them over, knowing well that they were wishing to see his bike.

"You want to try it?" he asked. "Maybe without the pacer."

"Do we!" exclaimed Elwood, jumping onto the track in one snappy leap like a grasshopper.

"Just once around. Take it slow, and stay on the inside."

A little wobbly at first, the bike carried Elwood along the hard floorboards, and before he knew it, he was managing to hold steady and increase his speed. The other racers called encouragement as they passed him, and he began to have a little confidence in his cycling ability.

"Keep control!" yelled Frank, noticing the increasing pace as his student made the turn. Elwood pushed one pedal and then the other with all the power he had, and to his amazement, he still held it together. Push, push.

Now I know why the Italians call Madonna "Poosha," he thought. *You must push and pusha to win.* This thought distracted him just as he was coming to another turn, but his legs kept pushing and pushing as the bike raced over the smooth wood. He cruised to a stop as he came back to where Frank and George were standing.

"You want to try?" asked Frank, looking at George.

"Naw, I'm not supposed to."

"Okay, sport."

"Can I try it with the pacer instead of George going?" pleaded Elwood, recognizing an opportunity. "I'll be careful." He looked at the motorcycle that was noisily idling on the track.

"I don't know, kid. Would *your* dad want you to?"

"I'm sure he would," insisted Elwood. "It would be fine." At this,

George looked straight at Elwood without any expression. "Wouldn't it, George?"

"Oh, yes. It would be fine," responded George, wondering what Elwood's father would really say to this. Somehow, he didn't think it would be fine at all, and he began to feel uneasy.

"Okay, kid, just once around," Frank said with a little hesitation. Then he guided Elwood and the bike to the edge of the track and held up a finger to Mario to indicate that the Anzani should go around the track once. As the pacer slowly came into sight, Frank pushed the back of the Mead Ranger to give Elwood a running start, enabling him to connect to Mario's motorcycle: "Off with you now."

Elwood had no trouble getting started because they were going very slowly. He just repeated what he had done before. As they gathered speed, however, he began to understand the trick of it. The pacer on the motorcycle was fencing the wind for him so that it was not as difficult to pedal.

What a difference! Pushing is so easy, he thought. But his presumptuous confidence led him to misjudge how quickly he would come to the curve, and he was unprepared when his bike hit the roller.

Wham! Crash! Down went Frank's bike with Elwood tangled up in it. Mario slowed to a stop, and Frank came running.

"You okay, kid?" called the pacer.

"I'm fine," said Elwood as he disentangled himself from the bike, and quickly got right up. "I'm sorry I banged up your bike."

"Nothing lost. I'm used to checking it out," Frank said, looking it over. "There doesn't seem to be any problem with it. You know you have to have patience when you're beginning and keep focused on the pacer. You can't get too close."

"I guess I learned that," agreed Elwood, red-faced at having taken a spill.

"You sure you're okay now, kid? I think you've had enough for one day."

"I'm just fine," said Elwood assuredly, noticing George's uneasiness and feeling some discomfort in his arm. "Besides, I think George wants to get home. Thanks very much. This was great, Mr. DiPaolo.

Good luck on Tuesday."

George was more than ready to go, so with withering looks at a trailing Elwood, he hustled ahead and slipped hurriedly back through the fence. But by the time they were ready to get on their bikes, Elwood was holding his hand suspiciously across his chest.

"What's wrong with your arm?"

"Don't know. It hurts. I think I might have broken it."

"Your dad is going to kill you. Can you ride?"

"I think so — maybe with my left hand, if you don't go too fast," Elwood said, trying awkwardly to get started. "Yeah, I can." They headed back over the train tracks and straight down Smithfield Avenue. When they got to Power, Elwood said again that his arm hurt, so they decided to rest. Two classmates were cutting through St. Francis Cemetery.

"What's up, guys?"

"We just got cones from Frank DiPaolo at the 'Drome," bragged George, forgetting all about their problem.

"We don't believe you, Big G."

"We did. Really. He's practicing for Tuesday right now. And Elwood got to try his bike."

"Yeah. But don't say anything. Okay?" interjected Elwood nervously.

"He fell. He thinks he hurt his arm." This from George, at last remembering Elwood's arm. "We're headed home. See ya." And the two pals resumed their trek on foot, pushing their bikes.

By the time they got to Elwood's house, both boys knew that Elwood was badly hurt; so they went right to his mom, who examined the way the arm was hanging and pronounced it broken.

"How on earth did you do this?" she asked.

"I fell off a bike."

"We'll have to go right to the hospital, Buddy," she said with an affectionate but urgent tone. "George, you had better go home, and we will let you know how it is later. Thanks for helping him."

"Bye, El," George said, wondering what the final act of this escapade would be.

At the emergency room, Dr. Sargent determined that the break was a fracture of the forearm, which he put in a cast. The patient was to keep the cast on for six weeks — and no bike riding. This would certainly "clip Elwood's wings," an old expression that his mom liked to use.

On the way home and throughout dinner, Elwood was much too quiet, and his parents knew something was wrong.

"What do you want to tell us, Buddy? Is your arm painful?" began his mom, with his dad looking over his arm again and everyone focused on it.

"You're a good athlete. How'd you manage to do this?" his dad asked.

"Well, George and I went to the Cycledrome to see the bikes," Elwood blurted out.

"I thought I told you not to go there."

"I know."

"Then what were you doing there?"

"Looking at the racers. And then Frank DiPaolo came in."

"The racer from Federal Hill?"

"Yeah."

"Yes," corrected his mother.

"Yes," repeated Elwood. "He bought us ice cream."

"I don't think ice cream broke your arm," insisted his dad sternly.

"Then he let me ride his bike on the race track, and I fell off it."

"Were you just on the bike, or on the bike behind the motorcycle?"

"Behind the motorcycle." At this admission, Mr. Euart rose, clearly upset.

"Why don't you and I go for a little walk." It was a command, not a question. Elwood felt a sick nervousness in the pit of his stomach at the look of disappointment he saw on the faces of both parents. He knew he had disobeyed them, and at this point, he wished fervently that he hadn't. He couldn't think of a single thing to say, so he silently followed his dad out the front door.

He and Dad walked down the block past the well-kept homes in silence, and it felt longer to Elwood than the whole day. Pretty soon they were back at St. Francis Cemetery. Mr. Euart headed in the front gate and turned toward the first lane on the right before making a left. The maple trees formed an arched cathedral over them as they trudged through the yellow and brownish-red leaves, and Elwood scuffed at them. He heard a couple of crows call to each other.

"You know where we are, Buddy?"

"At the cemetery."

"You know why we're going this way?"

"Because we are going to pray for someone you know?"

"Well, yes indeed. Right here," and they stopped in front of an almost life-size crucifix. "I think we need to talk about doing the right thing, don't you?" Elwood nodded.

"Why do you think I asked you not to go to the Cycledrome? Did you think I just wanted to keep you from having fun?"

"No. You said it was a man's place."

"That's true; but also because of danger. People sometimes get hurt by those motorized vehicles."

"Like me."

"Like you. I know that place is a magnet for boys. I've seen them hanging around after school."

"I'm sorry, Dad. I should have listened to you. I won't do it again," Elwood rushed the words out, truly sorry, and hoping to relieve the growing pain in his stomach that matched the one in his arm.

"And what do you think would be a proper punishment?" questioned his dad. There was a pause while Elwood thought about this.

"Not spending time with Big G."

"I don't think so. That would be punishing him. George didn't do any bike riding, did he?"

"No. He said he wasn't allowed to," answered Elwood, happy to put George in a good light, since his dad was just thinking about the accident, not so much about going to the 'Drome.

"Looks like you need to spend *more* time with George, not less. He had some sense. How about we take away your bike until Christmas. That'll give your legs an opportunity to get stronger so you won't fall off." He said this with a little smile and gave his son a shoulder hug so quickly that the "I love you" in it almost went unnoticed.

"Listen, Buddy. There are two things that a boy absolutely has to learn in order to mature: always tell the truth, and be obedient to your parents. Get it?"

"I didn't tell the truth either. I told Frank that it would be okay with you if I rode his bike behind the motorcycle."

"Hum. Now I am getting a better picture of this accident. You're not going to do that again either, are you?"

"Nope."

"I believe you, Buddy. The cast on your arm is going to feel mighty itchy in a few days, and that's going to be enough of a reminder to you to tell the truth. So let's get back to your mom, and we'll speak no more about it." And, with a few minor infractions, Elwood kept his word all his life.

Later that evening, George came over to see how he was doing.

"It's gonna be okay in six weeks," informed Elwood with a sour look. "And that's the end of Cycledrome adventures."

"Well, seeing Mr. Coppen, El, reminded me of the Steam Roller games. Maybe we can go to one of them with our dads. I'm getting to know the names of all the players from the papers."

"Like who?"

"The Cronins and Jimmy Conzelman."

"Everybody knows them."

"Yeah? Well, I'll bet they don't know Wildcat Wilson."

"Who?"

"Wildcat. His name is really the same as mine — George."

"That's why you like him?"

"Yes, and because he makes touchdowns. You'll see, if we get to go. He's going to be the best." George did not know that his prediction would come true, but not that year. They would have to wait until they were in high school to go to a Steam Roller game.

3

An NFL Championship Team

Three hundred strong, Elwood's sophomore class entered a brand-new Pawtucket Senior High School in the fall of 1927. The first multimillion-dollar high school east of the Mississippi, it was the pride of the city, sporting sixty classrooms, a 1,300-seat auditorium, and a swimming pool. Students dressed formally, the young men wearing jackets and ties, and they followed the Latin and English curricula of the day. Elwood did an adequate job with his studies, but nothing outstanding. His free time was spent playing in the school band, participating in the Boy Scouts, helping at home and at church, and palling around with his friend George. It pleased him that his band won the Class B title in the New England High School Band Contest.

In his junior year, however, things got exciting — not only for

Elwood and his classmates, but for all New England. Having established itself as a disciplined team, the Providence Steam Roller began to show that it could hold its own against any of the nine other football teams in the National Football League, including the New York Giants, the New York Yankees, the Green Bay Packers, the Chicago Bears, and the Detroit Wolverines. Each team carried an eighteen-man roster and played sixty-minute games.

Led by player-coach Jimmy Conzelman, the Steam Roller featured stars from Brown University, Connecticut College, Boston College, and Dartmouth College, with an all-pro center and two wrestlers, one of whom was an Olympic gold medalist. The schedule called for eleven league games, eight of them at home, and two non-league games. Their goal was to defeat the New York Giants, who had won the NFL title the previous year. George and Elwood had written out the schedule and posted it conspicuously in their homes as a hint.

The Providence NFL opener on September 30, 1928, was in the Cycledrome against the New York Yankees. Five thousand fans watched the Steam Roller move the ball 234 yards to the Yankees' measly 54 yards and win a decisive 20–7 victory, which motivated George to begin lobbying his dad to get tickets. By now George was a devoted follower of George "Wildcat" Wilson and his brother, Abe. He was glad that he had not pulled the deal off in time for the next game, however, because, although Wildcat faked a kick and ran for a touchdown, the Steam Roller lost to the Frankford Yellow Jackets 10–6.

The loss was rectified a week later by an easy win over the Dayton Triangles, 28–0, with Wildcat having another good day. Then the Steam Roller scored a second win against New York in Yankee Stadium. They were to return home for a game against the Pottsville, Pennsylvania, Maroons, so George and Elwood began an all-out, double-pronged effort, offering to do extra chores to earn part of the ticket price. They were successful, and their dads agreed to take them to the October 28 game.

"How do you think it will go?" asked Elwood as the four of them were approaching the familiar Cycledrome fence.

"I think the Steam Roller is going to win," said George confidently.

"Don't count your chickens," cautioned Mr. Costa. "This team used to play in the Anthracite League of a coal mining area. I think they might be tough for us."

"They surely could be," added Mr. Euart. "I heard that Red Grange called them 'the most ferocious and most respected players' he had ever faced."

"It's true they haven't been so strong as before their territorial controversy with the Yellow Jackets," Mr. Costa conceded, "but with Conzelman in the hospital having a torn knee cartilage repaired, I don't know."

"Simmons is out with an injured shoulder, too," contributed Elwood, "but we still have a good team."

"Wildcat is an All-American and knows what he is doing," defended George. "I still say we will win."

Sure enough, once inside they learned that Wildcat had taken over as coach and rearranged the team, putting Curly Oden, a kick returner and pass receiver from Brown University, at quarterback. The team went on the offensive right from the start. A later report of the game highlighted Wildcat's performance: He "threw a TD pass to Oden in the second quarter, with the extra point running the score to 13–0."[1] George was ecstatic. But not for long. In the fourth quarter, the doughty Maroons began a comeback and tried a final pass, but it was knocked down in the end zone, giving Providence the win, 13–6. The Steam Roller had now been victorious in four league games and had lost only one.

"What did I tell you?" gloated George. "I knew we could do it!"

"That you did," responded his dad as they dodged the exiting crowd.

"Bring on Detroit!" George and Elwood chorused with exuberance. And so, the fall progressed until the NFL race went into a tie.

At school, the boys spoke of nothing but the football game, and even the *Providence Journal* noticed that the Steam Roller was only two games away from the NFL championship. The team traveled to

Pottsville to beat the Maroons on their own muddy field, 7–0. There was just Green Bay left to face. The Steam Roller needed a win or a tie, as the second-place Yellow Jackets had three games left to play and could not catch up unless Green Bay beat the Steam Roller. A description of the end of the final game of the 1928 season, before a crowd of 10,500 at the Cycledrome, appeared later in the papers:

> Facing possible defeat, the Steam Roller took the kickoff and drove 72 yards in 11 plays, with a 23-yard pass play from Wilson to Oden scoring the touchdown. Gus Sonnenberg added the extra point with a place kick, and Wilson's well-placed punts kept the Packers in poor field position for the rest of the afternoon. The game ended at 7–7, making the Steam Roller the champion of the NFL.[2]

Big G had called it: his man Wildcat had brought the title home to Little Rhody, and everyone on Power Road congratulated him for weeks. The 1928 schedules posted in the two homes remained there all year.

* * *

In the winter of his junior year, Elwood joined the swimming team — he had excelled in that sport since his younger days at Slacks Pond — but his attention outside of school was on the Boy Scouts. He had been a scout since his elementary school days and was proud of the many badges he had accumulated. He understood the scout motto "Be prepared" to mean helping his mom with the care of his youngest sister.

Winnie's gentle care of her special-needs child, Ruth, was a model for all her children, especially the older ones. Throughout their high school years, they could be counted on to assist when things got overwhelming. Moreover, while it looked like her helpers were giving compassionately to Ruth — and they were — they were also receiving an understanding of the value of the human person, every person. Ruth was no "throwaway" child. Elwood called her "Roo." Sweet and always happy, she was loved by all.

When they came home from school, either Rita or Elwood took over for their mom. After peeling an orange and giving Roo some slices, Elwood would imagine one of the usual assigned chores as an adventure for the two of them. Together they would set out to explore the trash barrel, snip the overgrown hedges, or take their Airedale terrier, Prince, on an expedition. Since he loved animals, and their pet was usually in need when he got home, this last was Elwood's favorite. He, Roo, and Prince would have a walk around the block or head over to Big G's house.

Although he was not particularly artistic, on rainy days he would dream up craft projects for Roo to do, to give her the elementary-school experience that she would not be able to have. He instinctively knew that social time with the family was important, as was the love and respect they all showed her. In many ways, these little excursions and art projects brought cheer to the whole family. A loving brother, Elwood was conscious of a recommendation of St. Francis de Sales: "We should try to do the best we can."[3]

Sometime in his junior year, Elwood began working on becoming an Eagle Scout. Pawtucket Troop 1 was part of the Pawtucket–Central Falls Council until his senior year, when it merged into the Narragansett Council. From his youngest days, Elwood had followed a program of Friday meetings and Saturday hikes. At the meetings, scouts demonstrated their activities. They gave accounts of mowing, raking leaves, beating rugs, and caring for animals. Scoutmaster C. Maxwell Sherburne once gave a stereopticon presentation that traced the history of the troop. Sometimes the troop put on entertainments as fundraisers, making about thirty-five dollars. The traditional charge per person was by height: two cents a foot; over six feet, fifteen cents. They used the money to buy uniforms and to carry out various projects around the city.

Summertime was the best, because Elwood went to the Yawgoog Scout Reservation for a Scout Adventureland Week in mid-July. He entered through the gateway totem poles in khaki shorts, knee socks, and a straight-brimmed hat, looking forward to swimming. But first, there was a gathering at the flagpole and a salute, and then he was assigned to his tent, one of many in a wide-open field.

"Be prepared," a lanky camp counselor had reminded him on his first summer, as he rummaged absentmindedly for swimming trunks.

"They're right in here," replied a wide-eyed Elwood, stalling and nervous about being away from his parents. But he eventually found them, and he joined the other scouts in his tent as they marched in cadence to Yawgoog Pond. Each summer's experience under the towering pines taught him something.

"A scout is brave," he was reminded by a friend after a fall from an oak limb in the lower camp one year when he was learning wilderness survival and fire building. He had been imagining himself as one of Chief Yawgoog's scouts and had risked shinnying out too far. He had wanted to cry, but he didn't, and the bruise on his arm had lasted for the rest of the week.

"A scout is courteous," he had said laughingly to a camper who cut in front of him as he headed to Mass.

"A scout is reverent," the camper shot back, giving way.

In between the regimented walking and singing, the studying of insects and reptiles, the fishing and canoeing, the listening to night sounds and the traditions, Elwood had been learning how to lead his peers, until one day Scoutmaster Sherburne, noting his performance as a junior assistant, recommended that he begin to work toward becoming an Eagle Scout.

Already a First-Class Scout, Elwood had to earn an extra twenty-one merit badges in First Aid, Civics, Life Saving, Personal Health, Public Health, Cooking, Camping, Bird Study, Pathfinding, Pioneering, and Athletics and Physical Development to attain the coveted rank, one of 4,500 scouts in the country in 1929.

* * *

By his senior year, his sister Monica had joined Elwood at the high school, but it was a troublesome time. The stock market crash and the near-collapse of the economy had affected Pawtucket greatly, and companies that were poised to contribute to its employment had gone bankrupt. The Eastern Aircraft Corporation (EAC) on Campbell Street near What Cheer Airport was one of them. In August, it had announced production of three models of an all-metal Messerschmitt airplane intended for the German market, but it had needed to close down its plant, and those men and women eager for work were disappointed. With hindsight, though, the EAC bankruptcy was a blessing, as those very planes would have seen action against US servicemen in the European theater of World War II.

Like many Rhode Island families, the Euarts felt the economic pinch. At fifteen, and still in high school, Elwood began driving a taxicab in order to bring in needed funds. He must have given rides to some of his classmates, too, because they remembered his taxi in *The Pawsenhi*, the Class of 1930 yearbook.

In June, Elwood graduated from Pawtucket Senior High School in a traditional cap and gown commencement, but without any prospect of going to college.

4

FALLING IN LOVE

As he drove his taxi around Providence and Pawtucket, with an
occasional diversion to Cape Cod, Elwood was aware that most
of his classmates had moved on. A few buddies were at college; most
were pursuing careers in the trades. Some of the girls were taking
the trolley downtown for training as bookkeepers at Gladding's or
studying to be secretaries at Bryant and Stratton. *I'm completely stuck
in place,* Elwood thought gloomily. But just as the driving became too
repetitive to bear, his uncle Ed's construction business began to pros-
per, and Elwood was invited to join the carpentry crew. This pleased
him greatly.

On his first day, he was assigned to transport lumber to a lot on
Smith Street, near the corner of Nelson, that belonged to the Belliotti
family. It already had a pretty garden and a sloping front lawn, and
was about to become a gracious home with a front porch, steps with

turned banisters, and lattice skirting — the type of home that Uncle Ed had been building all around Providence. Elwood's skills by that time were somewhere between novice and journeyman, so he planned to approach the task with caution, conscious that he was a helper for Mike Foley, one of his uncle's assistants.

The early spring day was beautiful, with robins darting from nests in the evergreens and pink and purple hyacinths lending their fragrance. Mike asked Elwood to bring in materials from the "Ed Casey, Contractor" truck parked around the corner, and as he carried the two-by-fours, he became eager to test his carpentry skills. He knew he would have to learn how to set a porch roof, a tricky task that must be done right or the whole structure would collapse. Just as he was wondering how decorative Uncle Ed was planning to get, he heard a voice behind him.

"Well, who is this?" it said, startling him so that he fumbled with and dropped a box of nails. Tongue-tied, the best he could get out was "hello" to the strikingly lovely young woman who confronted him.

"I'm Maria Belliotti. This field is going to become my home," she continued, stating the obvious with self-confidence.

"Oh, I'm here helping Mike," mumbled Elwood in his low-key way as he stooped to pick things up.

"Nice to know you. We're looking forward to having a swing on the porch before the end of summer. We think it will be wonderful to be outdoors in the afternoons. Will it be done by then?"

"I hope so," said Elwood hesitantly, because he really did not know the timetable for the project and was thinking that the frame had to be raised long before any discussion of swings. He tried to think of something further to say, but was unable to get out any more; so, a little embarrassed, he hustled across the lawn.

"What's your name?" Maria called after him with a smile in her voice.

"Elwood. Elwood Euart. Ed Casey's my uncle," he called back, motioning to the sign on the truck.

"I'm going to tell my sister in the car," Maria laughed, heading toward Smith Street. "We want to have a say in some of the specifications. You will have to tell us what you are planning." And she disappeared around the corner.

Such was the inauspicious start to a friendship with the Belliotti sisters. In the early days, Elwood hoped that the job would just keep on going, and perhaps the family did, too, because long after the home was finished, new projects materialized that were not quite so urgent as advertised to Uncle Ed.

Often when Elwood stopped at the house to attend to something on his list, the sisters Maria and Adeline would greet him, and there was usually a tray of freshly baked cookies and a short time to chat. This continued into late fall.

One Friday, after he had completed a cabinet in the kitchen, Maria invited him to go with them to see a movie at the Majestic Theatre, and on another rainy afternoon, Addie suggested a trip downtown.

"Let's take the trolley to the arcade," suggested Maria. "I love all the little shops inside, and we won't get wet."

"What for?" asked Addie.

"I want to have a picture of all three of us. Don't you think that would be fun? Donna and Emilia went to a studio there, and said it was not too expensive. Then we can get something light to eat."

It was okayed by everyone, and the three of them headed to the large Greek Revival building that runs between Westminster and Weybosset Streets in Providence, the first enclosed mall in America. Bounding up its wide granite steps, topped by six ponderous Ionic columns, Elwood remembered his high school study of gods and goddesses and felt as if he were entering the Temple of Zeus.

After signing in at the registry in the atrium, they climbed two flights of stairs to the third floor, noticing the brightness coming through the glass panes of the skylight that spanned the length of the building, and running their hands along the fancy cast-iron railings.

They entered a shop with the sign "Bradford Bachrach, Photographs." On the wall inside were formal pictures of men and women and family groupings. A bouquet of fresh flowers stood on a front desk, and dark-blue velvet curtains screened off the back room.

On the left side wall, a Chippendale armchair was positioned on a platform against a plain background of medium value, and opposite it, a stationary view camera pointed at the chair.

When they entered the shop, a bell jangled, alerting a nicely dressed man with one blue eye and one brown eye, who hurried out of the back room.

"What can I do for you this afternoon?" he said with a smile. "I'm Mr. Milspaugh."

"We would like to have a casual portrait made," Maria offered.

"Certainly," Mr. Milspaugh responded, noting that they were wearing sweaters and jackets. "There is no charge for a sitting, and prices vary depending on size when you order from our proofs." Maria agreed, and the three took off their woolen jackets and hung them on brass hooks near the doorway, while Mr. Milspaugh went to get another chair from the back room. The sisters took their seats, and Elwood stood behind them. There was a momentary pause as they readied themselves and the photographer returned.

"If you are all composed," Mr. Milspaugh said, "I will shoot the picture," and he went behind the camera, which he treated tenderly, as if it were a musical instrument.

"Are we sitting correctly?" inquired Addie.

"You are. Except the gentleman needs to look this way," he waved his left hand, meaning Elwood's right.

"Just so, I think," said Elwood turning a slight bit so that he was facing Addie.

"Now hold still, look past me, and smile. Are you ready?"

"Yes" and "We are," they all assured him. And the man clicked the camera. This he did several times, while Addie wondered about his mismatched eyes and whether it was a suffering or a joy for him when he looked in the mirror. *Does he celebrate his uniqueness?* she asked herself.

When Mr. Milspaugh was satisfied that he had captured at least one portrait with all three looking their best, he proclaimed the sitting finished.

"We will be contacting you in a couple of weeks, as our plates are sent to the main office for developing on the fine papers we use," he explained, while the three of them reclaimed their jackets. Maria left her information with him.

Satisfied that the picture-taking had gone well, she directed the others to the sweetshop on the lower level, where everyone ordered a Laura Carr delight and an Eclipse coffee cabinet, the unique local drink known as a frappe in neighboring Massachusetts.

"Did you notice his eyes?" Addie questioned her companions as they selected a table.

"Weren't they wonderful?" asserted Elwood. "When he looked up, they were so expressive, especially for a photographer, who deals with color."

Maria was not so sure. She knew that Siberian huskies sometimes had mismatched eyes, but they were dogs. She didn't know whether she liked the phenomenon on a person.

"It contributes to his personality," Addie thought.

"I agree," added Elwood.

"Hum," mused Maria, still somewhat unsure. Elwood liked it that Addie could see things positively. It made him happy.

The conversation moved on to other things, and soon the three of them were back on the trolley, heading home after a pleasant afternoon.

Marveling at his good fortune, Elwood began to feel at home with the Belliotti sisters and their brother Buzzy. He liked their parents, Lena and Francis, a druggist, and began to drop by every so often on Sunday to spend a little time with a family not unlike his own in their love for one another.

As Christmas approached, there developed in Elwood a decided preference for Addie, the younger of the sisters, and they began to engage in conversation that, without excluding Maria, did seem to interest just the two of them. Both were readers. Elwood had begun to enjoy mystery novels when he was driving a taxi and had to wait for a fare; Addie had always been a good student. At first, they experienced the fun of concurring on the qualities of a given character.

One snowy Sunday afternoon, Elwood asked Addie what she thought of table-turning.

"Aha, séances," she laughed, spotting a clue from a recent novel. "You have been reading *The Murder at Hazelmoor.* The snow's not deep enough today for that mystery; it needs to be several feet."

"I'm in the middle of it now — the mystery, not the snow," admitted Elwood. "Mr. Sherman at the library downtown recommends Agatha Christie as the best English mystery writer since Wilkie Collins, and I'm inclined to agree with him, but I don't believe in table-turning."

"I don't either; it's crediting ghosts, but it makes a good story. What do you think of Miss Emily Trefusis?"

"I like her. Even though her fiancé is not a strong person, she loves him and will go to any length to get him cleared of the murder charge."

"Honestly, Elwood!" And at that, Addie huffed and rolled her eyes. "I caught that pun *person* for her fiancé, 'James Pearson.' You're not funny." She said this with a great smile, relishing the word play that was evident in the pun. "I won't give away the ending, but I do like the style of writing. There are little touches — like Detective Inspector Narracott's observation that Mrs. Willett 'always carries the war into the enemy's country' when she makes herself seem guilty by offering so many details. I know people who do that."

"And Mrs. Belling calling the police 'chuckle-heads,' " Elwood laughed.

"And the description of Sittaford House on the edge of Dartmoor, like Conan Doyle's *The Hound of the Baskervilles.*"

"Yes. I like the writing style too. Do you think newspapers are still giving away prizes for crossword puzzles and acrostics?"

"Not in this country. Retired military men like the captain may have won them from the London papers, but we won't. Don't even think about it, Elwood. You may like puns, but it takes a lot of reading to win crossword puzzle contests."

More and more frequently, life was punctuated by such repartee as this between Elwood and Addie, and they began to understand that they were being drawn to each other.

Christmas of 1931 was festive but simple, as it was set against the backdrop of a slow recovery from the national economic downturn. The papers were still printing pictures of long breadlines in New York and other American cities, with many still unemployed. In Rhode Island, the depression continued, dooming the city of Providence never to return to its former economic strength. Elwood's prospects did not improve; nevertheless, he turned over most of his salary to his parents to help with the necessities of life and prayed that times would change.

That didn't, however, keep him from squirrelling away something for Christmas presents. Hidden in the attic were quite a few unexplained parcels. There was a shirt from The Outlet for Rita, a bracelet for Monica, Chinese checkers for John, a Nancy Drew story titled *The Hidden Staircase* for Eleanor, a scooter for Len, and a stuffed monkey for Ruth — all to be added to Santa's gifts at the right moment. For Mom and Dad, Elwood had gone to The Electric Store to buy a radio, which he imagined everyone would enjoy after Mass on Christmas Day.

The Belliotti family of Smith Street attended church at St. Pius V, a congregation that the Dominicans of Providence College had established and moved into the chapel of a new school on Elmhurst Avenue. Most of the parishioners understood Advent as a time of preparation for the great event of the Incarnation, and even as presents were being made surreptitiously in many of the homes, families always refrained from setting out candles and decorations too soon.

Maria's activities were pointed toward the final adornment of the chapel. She knew that the friars were grateful for her artistic flair, and she had begun eying the greens they had cut and placed in piles behind the school. In a few days, she would help a couple of friars to assemble a great round wreath to hang from the ceiling, and smaller swags for the walls, affixing generous red bows and pine cones collected during a late-fall outing.

Addie had joined the choir, which met more frequently during December. To encourage her singing, her parents had recently borrowed a piano for the family and made a trip downtown to Axelrod Music for Christmas carols and *Heart Songs*. Family activities of cleaning, baking, and wrapping presents made for a great deal of hustle and bustle preceding the annual Christmas Eve excursion for the yuletide tree. Since this was a task for the father of the family, Francis enlisted Elwood to accompany him on an afternoon trip to "Waterman's Pond," as they called it then, to cut and transport a suitable evergreen. Upon their return with a six-foot spruce, the men were treated to cocoa and cookies.

That evening, Elwood repeated the task with the men of his own family. This time, the trip was not so far — just to an open lot a few blocks down Power Road, where the owner, a kind friend with a gentle demeanor, had requested that they "help clear things out."

"There is nothing like the smell of a fresh Christmas tree," proclaimed Mr. Euart, as he took a swing at the trunk of a perfectly proportioned little pine.

"Except maybe our house with a turkey in the oven!" exclaimed Leonard, already anticipating Christmas dinner.

"You're right, Len. Coming right up, as the chefs say," returned his dad.

"What would you think, Dad, if I went over to the Belliotti's house sometime tomorrow?" asked Elwood, changing the subject. "I have a gift to bring."

"For Addie?"

"Yes. It's a small gift, but I think it will please her."

"It's a book," guessed his brother.

"No. It's a widget," returned Elwood sarcastically. "Am I that predictable, John?"

'Well, if it's a book, I hope it has pictures. My art teacher says that I am getting on in painting, and it's something I like to do."

"Not in this one, I'm afraid. It's about knights and ladies. The Arthurian tales are interesting, and this one's by T. H. White."

"Yes, Elwood. It will be fine if you visit Addie tomorrow," interjected his dad. "You like her, don't you?"

"I do. We get along well together."

"Just remember that it's not time for you to be taking on any responsibilities, okay?"

"I know, Dad. I do."

The tree properly procured, the Euart family set about beautifying what everyone judged to be the most splendid tree ever. Decorations came out of a hinged wooden box that Elwood had made in seventh grade: five ceramic pieces made by Grandma, three starched crewel snowflake designs, a tiny painted wooden sleigh made by Rita, Ruth's yellow paper star, and several store-bought red and gold bulbs. The beautiful crèche they set up had been a Christmas gift years before from Winnie's brother, Tom.

The next day, the family went to the ten o'clock Christmas Mass, and then enjoyed a turkey dinner with mashed potatoes and gravy and lots of vegetables and pies, just as Len had imagined. After visits from aunts and cousins, Elwood was granted the privilege of driving the car to the Belliotti home, and he found excitement there, too. Relatives had arrived from Boston — one of them a piano player — and everyone gathered around for a sing-along, led by Addie. Elwood joined them, although hardly anyone heard a sound coming from his direction. After an hour of songs, some of them Italian favorites, Elwood began looking for a way to get Addie apart from the group. The chance arrived when her mom announced that cannoli had been set out in the sunroom.

"Addie, here's something for you," said Elwood stiffly as he held out the present. "It's by a good author, but I don't know whether Arthurian romance will please you."

"Oh, yes it will, El. I read Tennyson's *Idylls of the King* in school and loved it. Thank you so much." Turning, she gave him a kiss on the cheek. This completely overwhelmed Elwood, and there would have been an awkward moment if she had not immediately offered a present in return.

"What do you think? Can you stand another Agatha Christie?" she asked, holding out a rectangular parcel wrapped in green and gold paper.

"This is wonderful. You know that I love her stories, but what a couple of bookworms we are!" he answered with a laugh. The pure joy of the intimacy they had begun to share lent its sparkle to the exchange and to the rest of Christmas — and indeed to the whole season. Elwood had never felt so alive.

In the weeks that followed, he was changed. He thought about Addie incessantly. He caught himself humming some of her Christmas songs. He noticed things he had not seen before: a tiny rainbow cast by an ice prism, the shine of a handsaw caught by the sun, snowdrifts under the schoolyard swings. There was a kind of wonder that he could only attribute to Addie's kiss.

One day shortly after Christmas, Addie asked Elwood what he was going to do for his eighteenth birthday, and he launched into a description of Euart family birthdays.

"Usually Mom says something like 'It's your day, Buddy. What do you want for dinner?' and I always respond with 'cake and ice cream.' And there will be a few presents. But all day long, the decisions will be mine."

"That's what we do, too, but not all day." She didn't say any more at the time, but she and Maria had begun hatching a surprise. First, they asked Winnie if they could give Elwood a surprise party and whether she would give them a list of his friends and their addresses. Then they made invitations with a big letter *L* and a picture of logs (for "El-wood") on the front and sent them to Elwood's friends and family and their own friends and family. Soon the responses began to come in. Everyone thought a surprise was a great idea, especially the Ed Casey carpenters. Before long, the sisters had a very long list of attendees.

Since Elwood's birthday fell on a Thursday, the party was planned for the following Saturday evening, January 30. A foot of snow remained on the ground, but the weather was above freezing. No one had any trouble finding the Belliotti home. Elwood was under the impression that he had been invited for dinner, but when he got to Smith Street and saw the cars and trucks, he grew suspicious. And when he discovered the party decorations and beheld the many happy smiles on the faces of friends, relatives, and workers, he was totally astonished.

The living room was full of men in their Sunday best and women in soft, mid-calf dresses and marcelled hair. Among the Belliotti relatives, Elwood quickly spotted some he had met at Christmas. He was delighted to see his favorite cousin, Lucy, in animated conversation with his sisters Monica and Eleanor. Mike Foley was there with his uncle Ed and several carpenters as well as, of course, the host and hostess, Francis and Lena. He thought his mom looked especially pretty in a red dress with push-up sleeves, and his dad had already cornered George to talk football.

Addie and Maria welcomed everyone to their home, taking their coats and quickly ushering them to the side bar for soft drinks and hors d'oeuvres. One of Elwood's classmates, who had settled on the piano stool, kept the party full of jaunty melodies. And sometime after seven, a buffet dinner appeared in the dining room. There were not enough chairs for everyone, so the younger crowd sat on the stairs or on the floor of the sunroom.

A group of five — mostly Addie's friends — slipped into the pantry to plan a little skit as part of the festivities. They enlisted Rita to furnish content, and before long, they were laughing uproariously at their own ideas.

"Well, he loves animals, especially dogs and horses," contributed Rita. "There was that time he and George were at Greenville with Dad and found a horse that had broken out of his yard."

"What happened?"

"Elwood wanted to keep him, but Dad said he belonged to someone, and he had to try to find the owner."

"Did he?"

"Oh, yes. He and George went to three houses, and since he didn't belong to any of them, he determined that he was theirs."

"Now where did they expect to keep a horse on Power Road, not to mention get him there?"

"They thought they could tether him in the cemetery until Dad built a proper stall. Imagine that. We haven't any yard to speak of, but we've got to have a horse. Of course, Dad put an end to it by going to the nearest pub and finding out who the owner was."

"That's okay, but it's just silly twelve-year-old boys. Can you think of another one?"

"Well, he loves puns," put in Addie. "He is always saying things like 'They say a carpenter is known by his chips,' or 'Getting to know the tools was a riveting event.'"

"I know!" interrupted Rita. "He loves our dog, Prince, and usually walks him every day, taking Roo along. For a while, when he came back, Mom would always ask him whether Prince had wee'd, and Elwood always answered, "Yup, he definitely wee'd." So after a while of this, Mom stopped asking. Elwood would just yell, "Yup, he definitely wee'd" when he came in the door.

"I remember at school one time, Miss Boynton told him to take little Jimmy Eagan to the lavatory, and when they came back to the room, Elwood yelled out, "Yup, he definitely wee'd" right in the classroom. Jimmy was mortified, Miss Boynton startled, and I wanted to hide under a desk."

Everyone agreed that that was the one for the skit. Maria was chosen to read a verse of the nursery rhyme "Wee Willie Winkie" to start off, even though people would not get the connection at first:

Wee Willie Winkie runs through the town,
Upstairs and downstairs in his nightgown,
Tapping at the window, crying at the lock,
"Are the children in their beds?
It's past ten o'clock."

Then everyone was to sing the song "Ol' Blue," about a dog:

Had an old dog and his name was Blue.
Bet your life he's around here, too.

Every night just about dark,
Ol' Blue went out and began to bark.

Every pee was just in a rush;
Ol' Blue made a path to the white oak bush.

When they got to this part, Addie, imitating Winnie, was to interrupt the song by asking Elwood whether Prince wee'd, and then they would go back to the song again. They were to do it three times. Then they were to act out the school scene. George was to play Elwood and Maria Miss Boynton.

It started off just fine, even with an improvised accompaniment for "Ol' Blue," but every time they got to Addie's part, everyone got the giggles, so they had to start over. Finally, Elwood's classmate Charlie Swanson, who was a great tennis player, pretended to shoo them all off stage with an imaginary tennis racket, and they got to laughing so hard that no one could continue. Maria had to come out and tell the story as a monologue, to Elwood's great embarrassment.

The surprise party was such a rollicking success that everyone recalled it for weeks, and Elwood thanked the Belliottis over and over for such an unexpected sharing of happiness. But that happiness was short-lived.

In the doldrums of February, an outbreak of influenza hit Smith Hill and the neighborhood. No one knew where it had originated, although a circuitous rumor had it that people sick with grippe in Havana had been responsible for a summer epidemic in Puerto Rico that had connected to New York. Regardless, the students of Providence College experienced a mild epidemic, and soon many others also became ill.

With a tight chest and a cough, Maria was the first to feel uncomfortable, but the virus lasted only a couple of days, and then she was back to normal. Her mother experienced the same pattern, but when Addie began to get sick, it was more violent with a sudden onset of fever and muscle pain. She collapsed in bed on Valentine's Day, experiencing not only a tight chest, but difficulty breathing. Her family was worried because she had always struggled with anemia and was weak.

On the fifth day of Addie's illness, Dr. Henry Utter, who had diagnosed Maria, informed Francis that Addie's flu had become bronchitis and that they had to continue giving her fluids and keeping her warm; but within two days, she had developed bilateral bronchopneumonia, and was in serious trouble. To prevent any other germs from invading the area, the house was put under quarantine.

Elwood learned of Addie's distress from a mutual friend whom Maria had asked to let him know. Right away, he wrote a note that he left at the Belliottis' front door. Then, having heard nothing after three days, he ignored the quarantine sign and rang the doorbell. Lena answered and, with tears, told Elwood that they had thought that Addie's cough and laryngitis would go away, but instead they had gotten worse. She asked him to pray, and he promised he would. Never had he taken a request so seriously. He went straight to church and then began to ask everyone he knew to pray for Addie. But it was to no avail. The next morning, he learned that she had died.

He was shaken to the core, and his grief was so profound that he could hardly speak. Even though their relationship had lasted less than a year, he had already given his heart to Addie, and he felt as if a part of him had slipped away. Through the wake and the funeral, his parents tried to console him, but they met with stoic silence and sad eyes. In the weeks that followed, they witnessed his long face and empty evenings and knew that something within him had gone underground. But it was clear that he was not ready to tackle it. It was something that he kept to himself while continuing to work for his uncle, but there would never be another love in his life.

5

The 1938 Hurricane

By 1935, the Euart family had gotten back on its feet after the Depression, and Elwood was in a position to attend Rhode Island State College (RISC). With a sorrowing heart, he understood that it was time to get back on track both emotionally and academically. He had been encouraged by his cousin Lucy Casey, who had earned funds for nursing school by being a house mother at RISC, and her brother John was planning to apply. Grateful for his years helping to support the family, his mom and dad happily sent him off to the quaint village of Kingston, Rhode Island.

There is a tendency to think of a college education in personal terms as giving a payoff in later years: a good job, better health, and a longer life expectancy. And, like most college students, Elwood was thinking of these things; but this view of a college education as a private good is only partially true. It is a public good as well, because it increases the knowledge base, civic engagement, and the spiritual lives of the people in the place where the graduate finally settles. College has a bearing on what the student later does in life and on those whose lives intertwine with his.

As a land-grant institution, RISC was busy preparing students to contribute to the public good at a crucial period in their lives. There were three colleges: Agriculture and Home Economics, Engineering, and Science and Business Administration. The word *science* was taken in its broadest meaning, "knowledge," as courses were offered in both the arts and the sciences. In addition, the school sponsored a Department of Military Training and Tactics, the Rhode Island Extension Service, and the Rhode Island Experimental Station.

Because he loved animals, Elwood chose to major in agriculture; the course requirements included animal husbandry, rural sociology, horticulture, agricultural chemistry, and agricultural economics. He became active in the Aggie Club early on, becoming its president by his senior year. He also ran on the track team and played intramural sports.

Because there were few residence halls on campus, most men and women who did not commute to class joined one of the Greek houses. Elwood's was Rho Iota Kappa (PIK), and the brotherly camaraderie of its members and social events raised his spirits. He formed close friendships with men who had interests in common with him, especially H. Kenneth Higginbotham, John Patrick McCormack, and Angelo Marcello, who were all interested in military training, and he was chosen to be fraternity vice president in his junior year. The men lived in a white, center-hall colonial house with an open side porch, dark shutters, and dormer windows. Elwood attended Mass at the newly built St. Francis of Assisi church in nearby Wakefield.

In his third year, Elwood began a minor in military science and leadership, which included membership in the Army Reserve Officers' Training Corps (ROTC), a compulsory program that RISC had initiated at its founding in 1892. Three years before, in 1935, Congress had passed the Thomason Act, which permitted one thousand reserve officers to train with the Regular Army for one year upon graduation from the program. After that, fifty of them would be offered Regular Army commissions; some would administer the Civilian Conservation Corps camps; others would join National Guard units. Elwood was heading toward the Rhode Island National Guard. His courses focused on techniques of soldiering and the obligations of citizenship.

He, Ken, John Patrick, and Angelo became members of Scabbard and Blade, the college's military honor society for ROTC cadets. The society's goals were to preserve and develop the qualities of "good and efficient officers"; to prepare educated men "to take a more active part and to have greater influence in the military affairs of the communities" in which they resided; and "to spread intelligent information concerning the military requirements of our country." Its vision was to redefine "the standard of excellence for all military officers." District I, H Company, Sixth Regiment had been founded in 1927, and it promoted the Military Ball each year. Elwood would be elected treasurer of Scabbard and Blade in his senior year.

Although not a standout performer, he celebrated the track season in the spring of his junior year, when his team captured the New England Intercollegiate Track Competition held at MIT after an undefeated dual-meet season against teams from Brown, St. John's, Brooklyn, Manhattan, and Connecticut. His senior year, however, was destined to be one of unexpected anguish. It was a year that most of Rhode Island and Connecticut would prefer to forget, as the states experienced "one of the most destructive and powerful hurricanes in recorded history."[1]

Late one afternoon — shortly before four o'clock — three weeks into September 1938, Elwood was in the basement of PIK washing clothes, when, just as he was putting things through the wringer, John Patrick called down to him.

"Elwood, you have to come up. Something's happening. The sky looks funny, and the wind is blowing things over. We need to secure the yard." With that, Elwood hurried upstairs to help his fraternity brothers bring in the chairs and tables that had been left out from the night before. He noticed that there was an unnatural feel to the air: he felt a pressure in the atmosphere, there was a luminous yellow-green glow, and the wind speed was increasing rapidly.

He thought, *There is something wrong. A big storm seems to be starting.*

After he and John Patrick had moved the last long table next to the house, everyone went inside, but from the windows, they continued to watch the trees that were beginning to swing wildly.

In a few minutes, there was a crash as one of the campus maples lost a large limb just a few feet from the front walk. Everyone moved to the living-room windows, only to view a succession of branches falling and blowing as far as they could see. One tree was uprooted and flung fifty feet against a building.

While this was happening, Edgar Goff, a member of the school's newly founded Radio Club, took off out the back door, heading to the transmitting station. He did not know it as he braved the falling limbs and swirling branches, but the work that he and his club members would do in handling South County radio traffic for the next critical hours would be decisive for many people.[2]

Within a half an hour, Ken arrived home to report on what was happening at Narragansett Pier, where he had been with classmates.

"We saw ocean waves crashing over the seawall, their swells heaving up rocks bigger than basketballs. Sprays of spume showered the ocean walk and out into the road. More breakers were following right behind, taller than houses. This has got to be a hurricane. Some beach pavilions might even be washed away. It is certainly serious; I think we need to get away from the windows."

As the house president, Ken understood his responsibility to keep everyone safe. He immediately directed that they head to the basement, away from falling trees and debris. He asked Ed to grab some water from the kitchen and Angelo to raid the cookie jar and any boxes of cereal.

"We're going to have to sit this one out." No one argued with him and the silent order, as the way that the men moved away from the windows and down the stairs was testimony to the calm, dependable tenor of Ken's voice.

Outside, trees began to bend right to the ground and snap, bricks and mortar were tearing free from college buildings, and some roofs were being lifted hundreds of feet into the air. Elwood thought about Roo and hoped she was not scared in Pawtucket. Ken worried about his mom, dad, and brother, who he thought were at home, five miles from Westerly, very close to the coast. John Patrick wondered how far inland this storm would move. Every man thought about his family.

The Great Hurricane, as it became known, was the fastest-moving hurricane ever recorded at that time. It had traveled up the Atlantic coast at a forward speed of 70 miles per hour, and when it hit Rhode Island, its 121-mile-per-hour winds (with gusts as strong as 186 miles per hour) left six hundred or more dead, most by drowning, and thousands homeless. The beaches of South County were ruined when cyclone winds and water hit the continental shelf offshore at high tide during the autumnal equinox.

Around five o'clock, the wind died down as the eye of the storm hit RISC. There was an eerie silence: nothing moved, and all around, a wet, tangled web of broken limbs and branches covered fallen trees and damaged buildings. No one went outside, and after a few minutes, the great devastation and din began again. More trees were lost, power lines went down, and, as the wind began finally to lose its strength near six o'clock, "the air grew menacingly cold."[3]

When they were able to come forth from the basement, the men of PIK emerged to witness utter destruction. All roads were blocked by trees and debris, and it was immediately clear that there could be no classes for a while. Many of the men wanted to contact their families to learn how they had fared in the storm, but PIK was without telephone service. Gradually, however, people found ways to connect, and their reports were sometimes difficult to hear. No family story was sadder than Ken Higginbotham's.

His mom, Irene, dad, Harold, and ten-year-old brother, Jimmy, had decided that day to return to their rented cottage at Misquamicut Beach on the shore of the Atlantic Ocean. In the morning, his mom had called Ken's twenty-year-old brother, Stanley, to suggest that Stan and his girlfriend drive out in his 1929 Essex to join them after work. Then the three Higginbothams drove out to the cottage. As the wind picked up later in the afternoon, they went down to the beach to watch the breakers, but recognizing the increasing danger, they hurried back to the cottage to prepare to leave.[4]

As they drove away, they encountered Ken's girlfriend, Alma Bailey, and picked her up, but their car stalled in the rapidly rising water of the Shore Road. An account of the ensuing harrowing event was written by James Dodson and first published in 1988:

> Harold shepherded everyone out of the car and into a nearby two-story cottage. They were barely inside the door when an explosion of water chased them up the stairs. On the second floor, Harold smashed out a window. The water rose to their waists. He desperately helped Alma out the window, advising her to grab hold of floating debris. Next, he put Jimmy on a large piece of flotsam, perhaps a door. Then he turned to help his wife. Irene was nowhere in sight. He called her name desperately just as the house began to splinter. The next minute, flailing in the churning water himself, Harold heard Jimmy's terrified voice. Seconds later, Jimmy was thrown from his makeshift raft and disappeared.

Stan Higginbotham and his girlfriend, on their way to help, got to the Shore Road and had to stop because it was blocked by debris of bodies and ruined homes. They found Alma Bailey and then found Stan's father in tears at the Oaks Inn. It was getting dark, and they could only wait for morning. Stan drove back to RISC to get Ken before going to Stan's girlfriend's house, where "they huddled around a single gas-jet flame trying to keep warm."[5]

In the morning, Stan and Ken, Elwood, and several of the PIK fraternity brothers drove down to the Westerly beaches to assist the search parties that had organized to look for survivors. They began digging through the flotsam and jetsam of houses and furniture. "Stan found the body of his Sunday school teacher, Mrs. Bishop" and later the body of a friend's mother.

The men of PIK worked feverishly, carrying bodies and parts of bodies to workers, who took them to the local high school for identification. Finally, they learned what had happened to little Jimmy: "He was found unclothed, under eight feet of rubble, near Brightman's Pond." Stan said, "A doctor determined that Jimmy didn't drown. He died of fright."[6] It was a heartbreaking revelation.

Ken's college brothers did not give up. Like the true friends they were, they continued digging and hunting for his mom. Four days later, they found her body "not far from where her husband had washed up on Shore Road."[7]

It was a terribly sad time for Ken and everyone at PIK. Not only were they sorrowing for their friend, but they had witnessed death in a way that would leave its mark on them forever. And they returned to a campus of broken trees and scarred buildings.

In one of those buildings, Edgar and his crew of short-wave radio operators, who had been learning to observe weather patterns and relay the information to local authorities, got on the air immediately. As soon as the electricity went down, they knew that they would be the only reliable form of communication. As the storm progressed, and they began to recognize its magnitude, they broadcast to the world the news of destruction in Rhode Island. Then they took an active role in public service by notifying the Red Cross that South County was in need of help. The Red Cross assistance was critical as their "local disaster committees delivered food, clothing, first aid, medicine and shelter."[8]

When the search for missing persons began, the Radio Club students had sent out appeals for aid for the devastated coastal areas; they reported on bodies being discovered, the need for ambulances, and the loss of property. With 88 percent of the outlets in southern New England knocked out, the students had been the first responders in the early relief efforts.

Their work was picked up by "twenty-five amateur radiomen transmit[ing] from a room near the governor's chambers in the State House, relaying information between the state capital and the devastated coastal areas ... [who] passed on death notices, health updates

... and the course of relief operations."[9]

An exhausted Edgar returned to PIK to relate to Elwood and the rest of the brothers the situation as the Radio Club knew it: hundreds of people had died; more had been hurt; entire fleets had been lost up and down the coast; towns such as Misquamicut and beach communities such as Napatree Point had been entirely wiped out; and the state's inland timber industry had been irreparably devastated.

Edgar told incredible stories: a house blown across Charlestown Pond with a woman still in it, and the Bourne Farm barn and its cows taken in their stanchions. He had heard that some Providence motorists had drowned in their cars. A busload of children had been killed when their school bus was blown into Jamestown's Mackerel Cove. The Whale Rock's lighthouse had been swept into the waves, killing its keeper, and the Prudence Island Light's home had been washed out to sea with the keeper's wife and son.

There was much to pray for and many to be mourned. Fr. James Greenan, the friendly pastor of St. Francis, offered special services at the church for the sorrowing and programs to assist those in dire need.

Elwood's classes were suspended for a week as North Road was impassible and Davis Hall, which housed the infirmary and was the most recognizable building on the quadrangle, was a scene of rubble. Because of the downed trees and damaged buildings, there was little rest for the students, who, without electricity, cleared away debris and fixed the college buildings and the Greek houses. Elwood and his brothers worked hard raking, chopping, sawing, hauling debris, moving trees off the buildings, and seeing to damaged cars.

The men and their friends rose to the occasion: Just over a week later, everything looked fine for the arrival of the First Lady for the dedications of Mead Athletic Field, Rodman Hall, Quinn Hall, and Eleanor Roosevelt Hall.

When he graduated with a bachelor of science degree on June 12, 1939, Elwood was president of Alpha Zeta, the national honor society of Rhode Island's agricultural college. His class yearbook was dedicated to friendship, which the editors described as "one of the intangible, but real, benefits of a college education — the foundation of college life." His class adviser, Capt. Joseph William Kullman, wrote of college friendship as "a living ideal, having been forged by the heat of four years of mutual cooperation." The friendship of the fraternity brothers of PIK had surely been forged by the heat of the extraordinary events of their senior year.

After graduation, Elwood was commissioned a Second Lieutenant of Field Artillery in the infantry reserve, as the United States moved into its prewar mobilization stage. Ken put his ROTC training into action in the Air Force, eventually attaining the rank of full colonel. He married Alma Bailey, had two children before she died, and then married Madeline Delaney and helped to raise her two children. He was a dependable force at the Pentagon in Washington, DC, before retiring to Pawcatuck, Connecticut. Edgar married his college sweetheart, Shirley Sawyer; Angelo, an engineer, raised six children and is remembered by the many recipients of the University of Rhode Island memorial scholarship named after him.

At this point in America's history, there were more than a hundred thousand Army Reserve officers available for active duty, most of them having come through the ROTC system. Gen. George Marshall noted later that "without these officers the successful rapid expansion of our Army ... would have been impossible."[10]

It is likely that Elwood was recommended to be one of the thousand reserve officers to train for a year under the Thomason Act, but not one of the fifty chosen to become Regular Army, as he had been commissioned a Second Lieutenant, Field Artillery in the Rhode Island National Guard on July 16, 1940.

He was proud of his state's Guard, which had begun as a colonial militia called the "Traine Band" on May 13, 1638, in Portsmouth, Rhode Island. His unit, the 103rd Field Artillery Regiment, traces its origins to 1801, when it was called the Providence Marine Corps of Artillery (not connected to the US Marines) and was missioned to protect Providence merchant ships threatened by the French during the Quasi-War and by attacks of the Barbary pirates in the Mediterranean. The unit's first commanding officer, Lt. Col. Comdt. Seth

Wheaton (1759–1827), had served in the American Revolution. The 103rd had a distinguished history: It was active in the Civil War, mobilized in the Spanish-American War, fought in World War I as part of the "Yankee Division," and kept order in the state during strikes, floods, and hurricanes.

Elwood would have followed the protocol for all reserve officers. During the "closed season," December 1 to March 30, instruction was given from the *Field Artillery Training Memorandum* guide with as much practical application as possible. In the "open season," April 1 to June 15, there was outdoor training, commencing at 7:30 a.m. Training covered all Field Artillery Training Regulations affecting the duties of officers in a battery, including the maneuvering of a battery; care of guns, Jeeps, and machinery; drills for gunners; and instruction in military courtesy and pistol marksmanship. In the afternoon, there would be field artillery subjects for officers, with inspection by 5:00 p.m. Elwood was living at home and following the Rhode Island National Guard program. His family noticed his deep respect for his commanding officers.

On specified weekends and during annual training, the unit would travel to be able to use the munitions, especially howitzers, so that cannon crew drills could be perfected. The section chief would shout the order "Prepare to fire!" and the cannon crew members would have just a few minutes to do the specified job for these multi-manned weapons. Since all troops were cross-trained, the action had to be repeated many times, and each time, the troops could see the smoke from the rounds as they hit downrange. It was important for all the batteries to be together as a battalion for live-fire exercises.

These practice trips took on an immediacy as the war in Europe began to escalate. Elwood was commissioned a Second Lieutenant, Field Artillery, National Guard in the Army of the United States on January 3, 1941, when the Germans were bombing London and Manchester and the British Royal Air Force was attacking Mannheim. He was sent to the 68th Field Artillery Brigade Officer's School in Providence on January 27, and, just a month later, his unit was called into federal service.

He left Providence to join his unit, now a part of the 43rd Infantry Division, and reported immediately to Camp Blanding, Florida.

6

THE CALL OF UNCLE SAM

On January 14, 1941, President Roosevelt signed into law Executive Order No. 8633, ordering the 43rd Infantry Division of the United States Army, a National Guard Division known as Winged Victory, into federal service for one year. Immediately, General Order No. 2 of the 43rd Infantry Division canceled leaves and required soldiers to report. Those in the Rhode Island National Guard were relieved of local duty, activated in the federal service, and ordered to Camp Blanding. "A grateful Second Lieutenant Howard Brown was one of the men mobilized as part of the 43rd. At the time, he was working for The Brown and Sharpe Manufacturing Company in Providence and was making less than the $125.00 a month to which he was entitled while on active duty. Brown happily packed his bags and joined his division."[1]

Elwood and the 103rd Field Artillery Regiment, now a unit of the

43rd Infantry Division, arrived at Camp Blanding on March 19, 1941. It was a small National Guard post of 170,000 acres on the banks of Kingsley Lake in Clay County, Florida, that had been operating for just a year and a half as a training site for the infantry. Named after Florida's Lieutenant General Albert H. Blanding, who had served in the Mexican Border Service, in World War I, and had commanded the 31st Infantry Division, the camp had originally been funded by Jacksonville residents, but would eventually become the largest Infantry Replacement Training Center in the United States Army. The inhospitable camp has been described by soldiers as "hot to near suffocation" and "rife with sand fleas and mosquitoes." Indeed, "what does not bite or sting is a vegetable or grass that will scratch and tear at clothing or skin." The men of the 43rd found themselves in the position of having to build the camp itself. Arriving in the late winter, they encountered tents rather than temporary fixed buildings and found things in the final stages of construction. "Although civilian contractors did much of the construction, soldiers arriving there in the winter and spring of 1941 spent considerable time building rather than training."[2]

Since its inception, the post had been manned by the 31st Infantry Division, a National Guard unit from Louisiana, Mississippi, Alabama, and Florida called the Dixie Darlings. The arrival of Winged Victory troops from the New England states of Maine, Vermont, Rhode Island, and Connecticut set up a spirited North-South rivalry that resulted in the invention of a Mason-Dixon line running across the parade ground, which sometimes trapped soldiers trying to get construction work done. Complicating matters, the major avenues by the lake were named Alabama, Connecticut, Florida, and Maine, and the cross streets were also named after Northern and Southern places, setting up problems from the beginning.

"Y'all thank you can pass on Alabama, Yank?" a Louisiana soldier challenged Joe Hunt, a guardsman from Rhode Island and Elwood's friend.

"It's a way by the lake, Redneck, and I need the lumber pile," came a clipped response.

"With your lazy man's load. *Pas pour vous, couchon*," returned the soldier, blocking the way, confident of his Cajun lingo.

"What's that?"

"Not allowed for Yanks. Find a way on your own road."

"You keep this up, and Connecticut will be off-limits to you, Red."

Back at his bunk, Joe was curious: "Jim, what do you think *pas pour vous, couchon* means?"

"Haven't the faintest idea, Joe."

"One of the Rednecks said it to me today. Yesterday he called me an *âne*."

"They can't be good. Why don't you ask Marcel? He's a French-Canadian from Maine." Joe made a mental note to raise it with Marcel the next time they were together. He knew the soldiers had to endure one another as Blanding was a rigorous training camp:

> The sand was ankle deep in most places, and to circumvent this, the companies had to construct wooden "duck-walks" or paths to walk in. This meant that the only place to conduct close order drill was on the paved main streets. Moreover, the only framed buildings in the area served as Company headquarters, thus the troops lived in pyramidal tents during their stay. The troops often drew hole-laden canvas, and this was hung over a previously constructed wooden frame. These pyramidal tents quartered twelve men and were equipped with wood or coal burning stoves, usually located in the center of the tent.[3]

Elwood was housed in a two-story post commander's home overlooking the lake; the house was quarters for general officers. Like some of the other officers, Elwood had also been subjected to invectives spoken rapidly in French in a decidedly Southern drawl. One evening, as a group of "Yanks" gathered in their canvas tent, he questioned Marcel.

"Can you tell me what *poulets* means? Some of the Rednecks called the other officers and me that on Friday. Should we do anything about it?"

Marcel laughed. "Literally, it means 'chickens,' but in slang, it's 'cops.' To them, Yankee officers are lily-livered cops."

"Oh, and we were *couchon* and *âne*," interjected Joe. "What do they mean?"

" 'Pig' and 'ass.' They are really having fun at our expense. But they think we do not understand them and don't know that we know what they are up to. Let's beat them at their own game. Tomorrow we will be at the firing range. Whose squad will have the most Reds in it?"

"Mine will," proffered Elwood.

"I want everyone to learn these words: *tombez par terre*. It literally means 'fall on the ground,' but we would say 'hit the deck.' Just after we have finished for the morning, when Joe Hunt raises his arm, we will all yell *"tombez par terre,"* and they will think that they're in danger." When they had fleshed out Marcel's plan, each headed to his bunk, smugly anticipating the morning's revenge.

After breakfast, the assigned squads headed out to the firing range and took their positions. Practice began right on time and was fruitful, but at the end of the morning, just as they were leaving, Joe raised his arm and every Yank yelled, *"Tombez par terre!"* In fright, the Southerners, as a body, fell on their faces, and the Northerners guffawed and danced with glee. Even one of the Reds later admitted that they were "as nervous as a long-tailed cat in a room full of rockin' chairs." It was a sweet revenge that still finds an audience in the VFW halls of the North.

Basic training activities at Blanding included maneuvers, firing-range practice, and five-mile marches that soon grew to ten and then fifteen miles. Eventually they became fifteen-to-twenty-mile hikes to Keystone Heights, where the men camped on the reservation before returning to Blanding the following day. "Second Lieutenant Howard Brown described his training experience as 'intense' and believed that when the 43rd departed for the Pacific twenty months later they were 'quite well trained.' The only caveat he adds is 'At least, I can vouch for the artillery.' "[4]

Brown gave an amusing view of some of the artillery movements: "When we moved between camps in the states the artillery moved by motor convoy. We'd have stragglers. I suspected that much of the straggling was due to individual trucks stopping without permission at local soft and hard drink establishments. It was not too difficult to hide a 6x6 jeep."[5] John Higgins, an infantryman in the 43rd, was not so pleased with the training: "The training at Camp Blanding was only fair, at first we had very little of the normal equipment. '03 rifles, WWI helmets, WWI uniforms in some cases. Crew served weapons were WWI and in poor shape. Few trucks and shortages in all heavy equipment."[6] He does admit that the situation improved after "four or five months." A yearbook for the 43rd Infantry Division describes the Blanding experience as follows:

> When we first got there, the camp hadn't even been completely constructed. … We griped; we cussed out the sergeants; we talked about the officers. Gosh, when I think about it, it makes me laugh to remember how we yelled about the dirt, the sun and the heat. 'Course we didn't know that we'd be fighting in places that make Blanding look like an upholstered living room. Anyhow, we trained there. We learned about military courtesy. None of us could understand how that stuff could make us good infantrymen. My mom sure got a kick out of my salute. That was in July '41 when I went home on furlough. A lot of us got furloughs then.[7]

It may be that Elwood also obtained leave in July 1941 for a home visit. His unit had been building, drilling, and training for thirteen weeks and was about to begin the formidable Louisiana Maneuvers.

The troops were transported by truck and train from Camp Blanding to Dry Prong, Louisiana, arriving on August 5. The purpose of these exercises was to acquaint the men with tougher conditions and to give opportunities for the junior officers to lead. This was an opportunity for Elwood, but there were difficulties: rocky ground and swamps, forced marches in mud, blackout conditions for driving

Jeeps and trucks, and bugs — chiggers, red bugs, ticks, and mosquitos. Nothing was comfortable; nor were there any bombers available, and no proper material, such as mortars or anti-tank guns. Trucks had to substitute for tanks and tree logs for weapons. In the end, however, the men arrived back at Blanding more battle ready than when they had left. To their surprise, there was a new commanding officer waiting for them.

Born in Albany, Georgia, Brig. Gen. John Hutchinson Hester had attended the University of Georgia and the United States Military Academy. He had been a professor of military science and tactics and had seen action in Mexico. Promoted to brigadier general in 1940 while a member of the War Department General Staff (G3 — Operations), he became the Executive Officer for Reserve and Reserve Officers Training Corps Affairs. Hester was a kind man, fifty-five years of age, and devoted to the Army. His son relates a time when, as an infantry officer, he had asked his father's advice about transferring to a technical branch. With gentle firmness, the general did not waste words. "Son," he said, "the infantry is the 'Queen of Battles.'"

Having just headed up a training center in Georgia, Hester took command of the nearly sixteen thousand men of the 43rd Infantry Division in October. And in a month they were sent to Fort Lawn, South Carolina, for Third Army versus First Army Maneuvers, because they needed better air-to-ground coordination. The War Department appears to have been preparing the men for action in Europe's battlefields. In his master's degree thesis, "The 43rd Infantry Division: Unit Cohesion and Neuropsychiatric Casualties," Maj. K. Graham Fuschak, US Army, relates that "the Secretary of War held a meeting in his office with senior officers upon the completion of the Carolina Maneuvers, where the central issue discussed was tank tactics and equipment."[8] He concludes that "this issue reveals an orientation on Europe's open battlefields, less than a week before the attack on Pearl Harbor."

Elwood was promoted to First Lieutenant (temporary), Field Artillery, on his return to Blanding on September 6, 1941. He was missing his family and looking forward to a Christmas leave. But three months later, the Japanese attacked Pearl Harbor. He learned of the disaster from a flash over the radio and passed the news from tent to tent. Immediately all planned Christmas leaves were canceled, the one-year assignment was rescinded, and troops all over the United States began war preparations. And there were many soldiers: in a year and a half, the Army had grown by almost a million and a half men, as America was mass-producing fighting units. In addition, for the 43rd Infantry Division, there was the confusion of a reorganization of the National Guard Divisions.

In August, it had been announced that enlisted men over twenty-eight could return home when their year was up, and the 43rd had lost 180 soldiers. Then some National Guard officers were taken from their units to train others; and finally, twenty-five experienced officers over the age limit were reassigned to desk jobs, while the number of replacement officers was reported as "negligible."

The most difficult result of reorganization, however, happened in January 1942, with the move to an Infantry Triangular Division. The War Department had been administering the Army from a pattern of four infantry regiments within a division, but now changed to a pattern of three. For the 43rd, this meant the elimination of the 102nd Infantry Regiment, a battalion from Connecticut known as "The Grays," which had a distinguished history. As the brother militia to the original "Traine Band" ancestors of Elwood's Rhode Island Guard, the two units had fought together as far back as the American Revolution. They had shared the same woods at Pomfret and drunk from the Five Mile River. The sense of unity and trust among these soldiers was high, and their removal from the 43rd was an important casualty. History runs deep in New England.

Elwood was sent to Field Artillery School at Fort Sill, Oklahoma, in January 1942, and he completed his course in April, when he was transferred to Camp Shelby, Mississippi. His division had arrived there on February 19 and had become known as Hester's Happy Hustling Housewives, because it was primarily involved in the repair of infrastructure. They experienced some additional training, but only a single night movement. In late July, soldiers were granted leaves, and

Elwood went home to visit his family. On July 20, he was promoted to captain (temporary). Back at camp, a final inspection of the departing units followed an order for the 43rd to move from Shelby to a port of embarkation. It was early August.

The deployment order had been prompted by the situation in the South Pacific. The Empire of Japan had conquered New Guinea and was making inroads into the Australian territory of Papua. The first major offensive of the Allies, the campaign on Guadalcanal in the Solomon Islands, had just begun. And on August 4, the Navy destroyer *USS Tucker*, upon entering the harbor at Espiritu Santo in the New Hebrides — with no prior information given — had been torn in two by an American minefield explosion. Three of its crew were killed. The *Tucker* happened upon an "unknown unknown," something that had not been properly communicated to the ship's company. As Secretary of Defense Donald Rumsfeld explained many years later:

> Reports that say that something hasn't happened are always interesting to me, because as we know, there are known knowns; there are things we know we know. We also know there are known unknowns; that is to say we know there are some things we do not know. But there are also unknown unknowns — the ones we don't know we don't know. And if one looks throughout the history of our country and other free countries, it is the latter category that tends to be the difficult ones.[9]

This was a preview of things to come.

Elwood and his mates arrived at Fort Ord, California, by train on September 10, 1942, unaware of the "mistake" of the *USS Tucker*. They did not spend much time in the long wooden barracks on Monterey Bay, only enough to prepare for overseas deployment. They received personnel to fill vacancies and additional weapons and received practice in conducting small-boat landings. They did not leave with the main body of the 43rd, but remained behind with the 172nd Infantry Regiment for four extra days for additional amphibious training. The

103rd Field Artillery and the 172nd traveled by train to San Francisco on October 5, 1942, ready to depart for points unknown.

ELWOOD JOSEPH EUART   *Agriculture*

P I K, A Z

444 Power Road   Pawtucket

Track 1, 2, 3; Intramural Sports 1, 2, 3, 4; Aggie Club 1, 2, 3, 4, President 4; Scabbard and Blade 3, 4, Treasurer 4.

Elwood's senior yearbook entry, "The Grist," University of Rhode Island, 1939.

The Slacks Pond Boathouse (1944), painting by John F. Gallagher. Courtesy the McCaffrey family

Providence Cycledrome, with football game in progress. Courtesy ArtInRuins.com

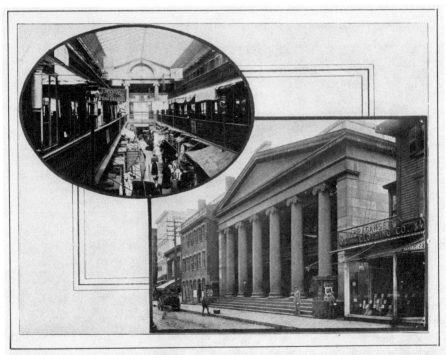

EXTERIOR AND INTERIOR OF "THE ARCADE."
This unique granite building, standing between Westminster and Weybosset streets, has a roof entirely of glass. It was built in 1828 for retail stores. Its six massive Ionic columns (monoliths) on each front are of Quincy granite.

Interior and exterior views of Westminster Arcade. Views of Providence (1900) printed by L. H. Nelson Company, Public domain, via Wikimedia Commons

Damage in Island Park, Rhode Island, from hurricane of 1938. Public domain via *New England Today*

Captain Elwood J. Euart in uniform. Courtesy the Defense POW/MIA Accounting Agency

31st Division Headquarters, Camp Blanding, Florida. Boston Public Library, public domain, via Wikimedia Commons

The steamship SS *President Coolidge*, built in Virginia by Newport News Shipbuilding in 1931. Photograph of an artwork by J. F. Newman, c. 1943.

Public domain via Wikimedia Commons

The beached transport SS *President Coolidge*, October 1942, Espiritu Santo.
Courtesy United States Department of Defense

SS *President Coolidge* rescue efforts. South Pacific WWII Museum, Vanuatu

A diver descends to the wreck of the SS *President Coolidge*. Christopher Hamilton / CHPhotographic.com

The Lady, a bas-relief still attached to the wall of the dining room of the *Coolidge*. She is the highlight of a visit to the wreck, and it is a tradition of divers to "kiss the Lady." Christopher Hamilton / CHPhotographic.com

An army jeep or truck, originally being transported on the *Coolidge*.

Christopher Hamilton / CHPhotographic.com

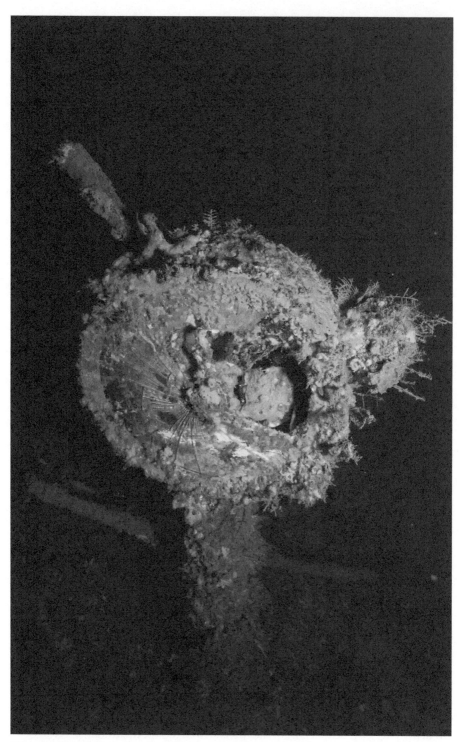

The ship's wheel. Christopher Hamilton / CHPhotographic.com

Memorial on Espiritu Santo, Vanuatu; the text reads, "In memory of Captain Elwood J. Euart, 103 Field Artillery Battalion, USA, October 26, 1942." South Pacific WWII Museum, Vanuatu; photo by Patrick Dancel

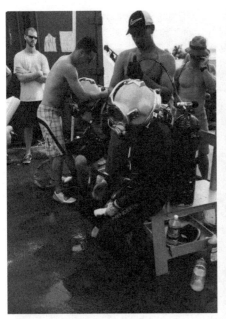

Defense POW/MIA Accounting Agency Underwater Recovery Team preparing to excavate Captain Euart's remains. South Pacific WWII Museum, Vanuatu

One of the many dives necessary for the operation. South Pacific WWII Museum, Vanuatu

Defense POW/MIA Accounting Agency efforts to recover Captain Euart's remains, 2016. South Pacific WWII Museum, Vanuatu

Captain Euart about to make the final journey home on a US Air Force C-17 aircraft at Santo International Airport. South Pacific WWII Museum, Vanuatu

Family and members of the military stand at attention before the 2016 funeral Mass in the foyer of Saint Maria Goretti Church, Pawtucket, Rhode Island.

Courtesy Rick A. Snizek/Rhode Island Catholic

Many of Elwood's family members attended the funeral, including several nieces and nephews. Courtesy Rick A. Snizek/Rhode Island Catholic

Father Robert L. Marciano, former chief of chaplains for the United States Air Force, celebrated the funeral Mass. Courtesy Rick A. Snizek/Rhode Island Catholic

Nephew John F. Euart Jr., of Atlanta, receives the flag from Capt. Elwood Euart's casket during the internment at Saint Francis Cemetery, Pawtucket, Rhode Island. Courtesy Rick A. Snizek/Rhode Island Catholic

Captain Euart's final resting place is near that of his parents, where he was laid to rest seventy-four years after his death. Courtesy Rick A. Snizek/Rhode Island Catholic

7

THE *PRESIDENT* COOLIDGE

When Elwood arrived at the Army checkpoint near Pier 42 at the San Francisco dock, Joe Hunt had not yet arrived, and Elwood wondered what was taking him so long. Thousands of GIs and a handful of nurses were milling around the wharf with duffel bags of winter clothes, bedrolls and footlockers, but he did not see any sign of the 103rd, so he set his things down on the pavement near the guardhouse and regarded the ship that would carry him to war: the United States Army Transport *President Coolidge*. At 654 feet, she was immense, perhaps half as high as the Industrial Trust Tower, the tallest building in Providence, and mighty in her pewter-gray vastness. He was overwhelmed. It seemed to him that the troops were just painted khaki toy soldiers in her shadow. He felt insignificant before something so great, and the idea came to him that the proportionality was not unlike the lowliness of man in the

81

face of the supreme authority of God. This first sight of the *Coolidge* inspired him to say a prayer — for himself and for all those who were assigned to her.

Dear Lord, he thought, *keep us safe as we head out to the ocean, and may I come back to my family.*

In a moment, he caught sight of Walter Wall with several others of the 103rd moving past the MP sentry toward the other end of the wharf, and when he turned, he saw Joe in uniform with his helmet and rifle.

"Were you waiting long?" Elwood asked him.

"Nope. Just got here. Take a look at this beauty!"

"Whoa, kiddo! That's one big sailboat!"

"Well, it's got to navigate one big pond."

"Sure thing. You still think we're going to Alaska?"

"Why else would we get winter clothes? Just like the Army to send us to Florida and Mississippi for training when we're headed to Alaska," Joe chuckled, glancing around the pier, which was rapidly filling up with men and a few women.

"Look at the number here," Joe commented. "There must be a couple of thousand."

"More than that, I think."

"And what do you know about the ship? Will she float?"

"You're not funny," Elwood replied. "I know that she was built as a commercial ocean liner by the Newport News Shipbuilding and Drydock Company and first owned by the Dollar Steamship Line. From 1931 to 1941, she was a trans-Pacific passenger ship. When we were training at Camp Blanding, the government took her over from the American President Line and converted her to a troop ship. She's been sailing the trans-Pacific run, carrying Army and Navy men and supplies to the US bases and bringing evacuees back home. For a liner, she's fast. Her port of registry is here in San Francisco."

"I remember seeing a photograph in the papers of Mrs. Calvin Coolidge christening this ship about ten years ago," contributed Joe.

"She had a sister ship, the *SS President Hoover*, that ran aground on an island off Formosa."

"That reminds me: Why did the one-eyed captain run his ship aground?"

"Really, Joe. Is this one of your purposeless jokes?"

"He didn't have any depth perception."

"Okay. Stow it. Let's catch up with the others. I saw Walter heading this way."

As the two of them moved on down the pier past some civilians behind a barricade waiting for the send-off, they considered the floating hotel that they were about to board.

The *Coolidge* was the largest merchant ship of her age, and she *was* fast for a liner: even with a thirteen-thousand-ton hull, her speed could exceed twenty and a half knots. She had crossed the Pacific westbound in just over nine days.[1] There were twenty lifeboats,[2] and what had once been luxury accommodations for 988 guests[3] had been expanded to serve 5,000 soldiers. Elwood and Joe were to discover that sleeping arrangements were no longer luxurious — rather, many of them were tiers of bunks in the hold and about the ship. The lady had electricity, radio, and air conditioning, but not in the hold. One of her swimming pools had been removed, and no longer were the library, the sound picture theater, the writing room, or the musicians' gallery available for the stylish class, because there was no stylish class anymore. In her salad days, the *Coolidge* had carried such celebrities as Baron Henri de Rothschild, Mrs. Spencer Tracy, and silent-film star Mary Pickford, and had sported such extras as a shipboard stock exchange, a shopping arcade, and a beauty salon.[4] These had been reassigned. But she was up to the task of moving army men and machinery: she had guns mounted fore and aft, and she had military glamour, having recently brought Gen. Douglas MacArthur home from Manila.

Within minutes, the two heard the grinding sound of a belt line railcar making its way down the wharf toward the waterfront. Forty enlisted men, a sergeant, and a second lieutenant of the 172nd infantry, who had just completed their basic training at Fort Ord, had been sealed within it for two and a half hours. The car had detached from the Daylight Limited that ran from Los Angeles to Seattle and then moved right onto the rails that ran to Pier 42. An MP cordon stood waiting to guide the troops up the gangplank. Shortly, their duffle bags, footlockers, and bedrolls were swung aloft in a cargo net as each troop was checked off the ship's manifest.

"We'd better hustle down to the 103rd," urged Elwood, and they set off toward midships, where the 172nd Combat Team, under the command of Col. James A. Lewis, was gathering. In no time, they divided into four contingents: the 172nd Infantry Regiment, the 103rd Field Artillery Battalion, a platoon of engineers, and a medical company. The infantry organized again, and all proceeded to be checked in at the gangplank.

Once on board, all the troops scrambled to find their sleeping quarters. The enlisted men found themselves packed tightly into every space imaginable, especially in the holds. The ship was also carrying ten thousand tons of cargo, mostly war material, such as Jeeps, tanks and munitions, and medical supplies destined for Guadalcanal — including a great quantity of quinine for malaria.

Joe was assigned to a three-tier bunk on D deck with Elie Shue above him and Edmund La Rue below. Elie was a quiet man with no taste for card games. Years later, Joe learned that he kept a small New Testament in his left shirt pocket and that, as he faced gunfire on Okinawa, his life was spared when a bullet hit the Bible, right at the words "Another time Jesus went into the synagogue, and a man with a shriveled hand was there" (Mark 3:1). But at this moment, Joe was simply grateful for his welcoming handshake.

"Name's Elie Shue. Glad to know you."

"Joe Hunt. You're not a loafer, are you? Just kidding. You probably get that all the time."

"Nope. It's usually something about boots where I come from."

"Where's that?"

"Vermont."

"Bring any maple sugar with you?"

"Wish I had. Where're you from?"

"Rhode Island, like Ed. It's a state made up of coastline."

"Now that's a place that's so small nobody can find it.'

"You got us there."

Joe and Ed talked some about home, before being branded "lobsters." Pretty soon Joe was keeping everyone in earshot well entertained with homespun humor and tales of the sea. This was a good distraction, as their main-deck lodging left a lot to be desired. They were aft in an area originally planned for steerage passengers and cargo. The canvas bunks were crammed together so tightly that they were just two feet apart. There were no pillows, so they used their packs.[5] If any of the men needed to use the head, they had to go up to the promenade deck, where there were long lines of soldiers waiting for the three rows of toilets — thirteen, thirteen, and fifteen — that had only an excuse for a wooden partition between them, no privacy at all. They would quickly learn to get going to the head long before it was truly necessary. At noon, some temporary rations were passed out, and Joe, Elie, and Ed went topside to get a view of the harbor.

Elwood's first experience was different. As a captain, he was berthed in a cabin on C deck not far from the main mess. A former single-passenger stateroom, it had become a nesting box for four officers, but the accommodations were a lot better than the enlisted men's quarters. Even though all of them could not stand up at the same time and stretch their wings without elbows ending up in someone else's ribs, there was air conditioning and a general sense of well-being. They knew that the discomfort would last only a few days.

Elwood regarded his new companions. He knew 2nd Lt. Howard Brown from their Rhode Island weekend maneuvers and from their days at Blanding. Whether or not he was related to *the* John Nicholas Brown, Howard's aristocratic presence in a group always prompted a lot of ribbing about the dark side of that family's affairs — smuggling whiskey and the slave trade — but he took it good-naturedly and lived out his reputed legacy by always being game for a few drinks.

First Lt. Charles J. Stephenson of Vermont, the Green Mountain State, had relocated from New York City. Used to managing students in the teeming immigrant neighborhoods south of Fourteenth Street, he spoke with a clipped authority that could be off-putting. His pace was faster than that of the other men, so it seemed that he was always in a hurry, but he was a hardy soul who put up with things that would annoy most others.

A baseball fanatic, 2nd Lt. Charles "Chuck" McCary knew every statistic of every player in the American and National Leagues. He was a Red Sox fan, and his favorite player was Jimmie Foxx, who had disappointed him lately. Chuck had hoped that 1942 would be the year that the Sox would take the pennant, but they had come in second to the ever-dominant Yankees, so he rooted for Stan Musial's Cardinals to squash them like a bug in the World Series, which they had done just the day before. He felt vindicated. Recently he had begun to direct his fine memory toward the theaters of Europe and Asia, learning the names of most of the countries, their capitals, and their natural resources. He figured he might be needing geography stats more than baseball ones in the coming months.

"Any of you know who's sailing this bucket?" Brown asked, although he had heard a name tossed around on his way up the gangplank.

"I think it is Capt. Henry Nelson. Two guys I was standing with said he is well-respected — could have retired, but wanted to do his patriotic duty," said Elwood.

"He's sixty-three, so we can call him Grandpa." This from Chuck, who, responding to the numbers, was busy stowing things under his bed.

"Well, a Chinese-American cook I spoke to in the lobby told me that the Merchant Marine crew has had a lot of experience, having crossed the Pacific previously to such places as Hong Kong, Shanghai, the Philippines, Melbourne, Bora Bora, and Fiji."

"It looks like the trip, while not comfortable, will at least be expeditious."

They were interrupted by a messenger for Elwood. He was to report to the ship's dining room on C deck as soon as he had his gear in place. This was not a surprise — Colonel Lewis had informed him that he would be the mess officer in charge of the enlisted men's dining hall from morning to night.

Three times a day, hundreds of soldiers collected in the area that had been converted from a first-class dining room and other rooms to a mess hall with chow that they hoped would be tolerable. They were under no illusions — most of them having lived through the cooking at Shelby and Blanding — but they were expecting something substantial at least, and most of the time, they were not disappointed. Unlike some cooks on later troop ships, such as the *Cape Horn*, which served up pig swill and soggy bread, the *Coolidge* chefs did their best to satisfy the soldiers. But not everyone could be seated at one time, so there were three half-hour sittings for each meal.

Elwood proceeded to the mess hall and found that hundreds of long tables had already been set up. He introduced himself to the kitchen staff, who seemed to be from various Asian countries as well as the United States, and saw that there were already many men on KP duty, and their helpers were getting large metal serving containers and big serving spoons ready. He knew that during meals his job would be to stand at the end of the serving line to ensure order and keep the men from badgering the servers for more rations. The food that was being prepared smelled good, maybe even the very rare beef they called "tiger meat," so he was pleased.

At 1700 hours, the first sitting of men began to arrive. During prep time, Elwood had heard the loudspeakers send groups into companies, and that is how they arrived. He directed them toward the serving line, where they got their supper and headed to the tables to eat and converse. Some who had missed the temporary rations because of late connections were especially hungry for supper. Those who groused about it he put at the head of the line. The men did not have much time; they had to finish eating and return their trays by 1720. The next sitting arrived at 1730 and the third at 1800. Although Elwood knew that some of the officers on B deck were served in their staterooms, it still amazed him that five thousand enlisted men could be fed in an hour and a half!

As the cleanup crew was working around the hall, Elwood saw a familiar face. In came soft-spoken Father Mahoney, the chaplain of the 172nd Infantry Division, who wanted to discuss arrangements for Mass on the following days. They agreed that, to allow for a short

Communion fast, the best time would be in the afternoon, because the hall would be given over to instruction and drills in the mornings. Elwood agreed to have everything cleared and ready for Mass by 1500 hours each day. In a few minutes, a messenger came from Col. Dinsmore Alter, who was in charge of the troops, reserving the hall for 900 hours. So, saying "good night" to Father, Elwood found a quiet table to make out a schedule for the mess hall.

Just after midnight, quietly and without fanfare, the *President Coolidge* passed under the Golden Gate Bridge and out into the Pacific. The order to extinguish all lights was given, and the ship began to pick up speed, zigzagging to avoid Japanese submarine torpedoes. This evasive tactic was used by troop ships throughout the war, as the slow, unaccompanied transports had few effective weapons — the *Coolidge* had one five-inch and four three-inch guns — and could easily be picked off. She was heading west and, since many of the men had been issued winter gear, would surely turn northward after a few days. Her destination was generally believed to be Alaska.

It didn't take long for the enlisted men to decide that Elwood was an okay officer. When he could, he tried to see that everybody got enough to eat and was well treated. He had had his first test at the last supper sitting earlier, when the mess was buzzing with chatter: he had watched six men come in together, put their trays down on the long table, and begin to eat.

"Hey, troop. I heard you were on this kettle," one soldier greeted another.

"Jack, good to see you again."

"How's your brother Caleb? I was with him in Atlanta last year. We had a blast." As this conversation was taking place, the troop's friends were stealing his tray, passing it hand to hand under the long table and on to the next table and to the next until it was out of sight.

"Sure good to see you here. Take care now." Jack finished by shaking hands.

"Nice to see — whoa! Where's my food? This is not good. The line's closed."

"Search me," one of his friends said with a suspicious smirk.

"What food?"

"You ate it. Don't you remember?"

"Nah. You guys took it. Some friends you are," grumbled the troop as he snatched a buttered roll from one of their trays.

From his position at the end of the room, Elwood had seen the tray magically disappear, and he headed to the end of the row of tables.

"Anyone know where the troop's tray ended up?" Silence. "Just be sure that it finds its way to his bed before dark," he announced. "We don't want to have any soldiers passing out from hunger on our ship now. Do we?"

And just as magically as it disappeared, the tray reappeared.

8

ON THE HIGH SEAS

The next morning, promptly at 900, 930, and 1000 hours, three
contingents gathered for mess-hall sessions to hear Colonel Alter
give instructions with a bullhorn. Elwood had everything ready. He
regarded the colonel, who was of medium build and walked with a
long stride that made his shoulders swing, giving the impression that
he was trudging along.

First, the colonel ran down key items on his list: lights-out strict-
ly enforced; no smoking after dark; nothing thrown overboard; no
sitting on rails. These were things the men and women could readily
understand, as there was the threat of Japanese subs constantly over
their heads. They could see that all the portholes had been painted
black, so that no light could be detected from the outside and give the
ship away. They knew that little was supposed to happen after dark,
and if it *was* necessary to do something, doors were to be closed to

contain the light.

The colonel prohibited cigarette lighters and matches because they would flare up and could be seen. He assigned units to specific quarters and said that troops were not to wander about the ship.

Elwood learned that he had to pay close attention to the day's garbage from the galley and elsewhere. His boys could throw it overboard at only one time, just after dark, so the Japanese would not be able to detect the direction that the ship was heading, as they would not see the garbage until the next morning, when the ship was far away. Additionally, no one was to throw anything overboard for any reason, or he would risk being sent to the brig. Elwood thought that this would be hard on some smokers, who were used to tossing around their cigarette butts and packs of Camels and Lucky Strikes.

Since many of the men had not been on a ship before, they were warned not to sit on or horse around near the railings, as they could easily fall overboard. In his memoir, *The World Is My Home*, James A. Michener recalls how this message was not heeded by a sailor on his troop transport, even though the commanding officer had warned them: "Do not, I repeat, do not, sit on the protective railing that goes around the ship or act up when in its vicinity. Because I promise you that if you fall overboard our captain has orders to continue on course and not stop dead in the water so that a Jap submarine could pop us. I repeat, we will not stop or double back to pick you up." Michener reports how a loudmouthed sailor did fall off the railing, "As warned, we sailed straight ahead, and as his anguished screams grew faint, we felt that the war had overtaken us and was grappling for us with clammy hands."

Colonel Alter assured everyone that if they kept to the rules, they would have a smooth trip. Since the weather was sunny and clear, and the sea calm, they could spend time on the deck exercising and discussing sports and the war. They were to wear their life jackets at all times. There would be unannounced abandon-ship drills occasionally during the trip, so the troops would be divided into groups and assigned lifeboat stations with two crew members for each station to assist the troops into the lifeboat and lower them into the water.[1] After each of Alter's meetings, Elwood reorganized the chairs that had been set askew and asked the colonel whether he needed anything.

In the afternoon, after Mass, Father Mahoney suggested that there would be fewer at supper sittings that evening, because many of the troops were feeling seasick. And sure enough, the numbers were down considerably. Some of the men stayed in their bunks; others sought out the fresh sea air on deck; one found solace in a lifeboat. The night sea was fairly rough, so many struggled to keep their stomachs stabilized, especially those on the top bunks.

Thankfully, the morning dawned with pleasant weather and only occasional ocean swells, so most of the men returned to the mess hall. It was announced that Col. Alter had named Lt. Brown to a special project: the return of the winter clothes. Even though the men *had* been aware that the ship had not turned northward, as they had expected, it came as a surprise when they heard over the ship's radio, "Now hear this! Now hear this! All personnel will proceed to sleeping quarters, retrieve all winter gear, and parade on the upper decks." The men arrived on the upper decks to find signs for various sizes of overcoats, pants, wool jackets, and gloves posted on the cabin doors, and they were directed to throw the appropriate garment into the appropriate room.[2] Then they were issued summer uniforms. So much for Alaska.

At this, rumors began to spread. It was remarked that the weather was getting considerably warmer. Someone had overheard something about going to a destination called White Poppy, but no one knew what that meant.[3] There was much talk about the war in the South Pacific.

White Poppy was the code name for Nouméa in the French territory of New Caledonia, the headquarters of the commander of the South Pacific, Adm. William F. Halsey; so, when one of the officers figured that out, they knew that they were heading toward the battlefront. It was a critical time.

When the officers gathered for supper, McCary commented, "There was conflict near the Solomon Islands last May when we won the Battle of the Coral Sea. That was *west* of New Caledonia," and everyone nodded, because they all knew about that.[4]

"It was just ten weeks ago that we took Guadalcanal from the Japanese, too," added Elwood. "I expect that the men who fought there are ready to be reinforced with men and supplies." They all grunted agreement.

"A cook who sailed to the Pacific ports told me that there are staging bases in the New Hebrides," interjected Brown with new information. "They put them together in a great hurry."

"Really! Now that's interesting."

Such chatter was not far from the mark. Troops and material had begun to come through Nouméa to the Solomon Islands, along a pathway that ran overland from Detroit to San Francisco and oversea to Nouméa and would later become known as "the train," the supply-line route to the battlefront. The men and women of the *Coolidge* were in the first car behind the steam locomotive.

It was no surprise to the officers when target practice was announced the next day. Lt. C. Craig Hosmer, US Navy Reserve, who oversaw the Armed Guard Unit assigned to the ship, had planned activity for the ship's battery. Something like a dark "killer tomato" target was dragged by rope from the stern of the ship. One of the three-inch guns that was mounted on the stern deck was trained on the target, and when it went off with a great roar, the steel deck pulled and shook as if it were about to come apart. The enlisted men were ordered below deck when the practice started, but the mere fact of the practice somehow gave everyone confidence.[5]

And so they proceeded across the ocean, with pleasant breezes and sunshine, daily exercises on deck and pretty good food. Except for the secret of exactly where they were headed, the trip had become monotonous. Then, one day, they crossed the equator, and every enlisted man knew that he was headed for the South Pacific.

Of course, there was the requisite crossing ceremony. The swimming pool had been filled with salt water into which Elwood and his boys had dumped garbage from the kitchen for the special event. Each company or unit selected a second lieutenant as its representative and told him or her to dress only in shorts or a bathing suit. This was Joe's idea, passed along the line of command to a sergeant.

Lieutenant Stephenson, the other lieutenants, and one nurse were blindfolded and pushed into the pool. Some soldiers prodded them to the end, where King Neptune and his court (no one owned up to how *they* were dressed or not dressed!) fished them out and gave them five lashes. As many enlisted soldiers as could fit in the area were on hand to watch the festivities, and they passed an account on to their mates who were so far behind that they could not see. There was laughter and foolery, and the event was great for morale. Afterward, Captain Nelson invited "the initiates" to dinner, which included some bourbon,[6] and everyone was presented with a fancy certificate.

The *Coolidge* stopped for a few days on Canton Island to correct engine problems, and Milt Staley (who would, later in the war, be awarded the Silver Star for combat gallantry) and some other troops watched a flight of American fighter planes take off. In a few days, the ship's radio news mentioned an American base in the New Hebrides that had been shelled, and when the newsman spoke of it again, McCary and those in the know began betting that the ultimate point of debarkation would be the New Hebrides.[7]

Many a thoughtful person had begun to speculate about the war zone. What would it be like to be shot at or to have a grenade explode nearby? Elwood had an opportunity to check in to Joe's bunk in the hold, and they had spoken in oblique terms. Behind his comic exterior, Joe was apprehensive. His friend was sure of it and suggested that he have a chat with Father Mahoney. He told Joe that more and more men and women were showing up for Mass and having chats with Father afterward. He said he was going to Mass and Holy Communion every day and had signed up to be "adopted" by a child in the states: The child would pray for him if he said a certain prayer every day. Elwood gave Joe the Soldier's Prayer:

O God of Love, make me a soldier
 worthy of the Great Cause for which we fight.
Give me strength when the going is hard.
 Give me courage when danger is near.

In Thee I place my trust.
Lead me through the perils of this war
    to the Better World to which I have dedicated my life.
But if the service of Thee and my Country calls for the
    sacrifice of my Life,
I only ask, dear God, that Thou be with me at that moment,
    confident that Thy Peace awaits me in Eternity!

Joe took the prayer, and listened respectfully, but made no response to Elwood's urging.

On Tuesday, October 20, the ship arrived at Nouméa for a four-day layover. When the troops saw their winter clothes being offloaded in cargo nets, they were mighty unhappy to learn that they were required to remain on board.

"What is this? We have to stay put?" complained Ed as he lay in his bunk in the extremely hot, humid hold.

"I was hoping for a little sightseeing in this paradise. You know, beautiful legs beneath the palm trees," interjected Joe with a mischievous smile. "A tropical paradise with the prettiest girls, agate blue water, and fine Polynesian food."

"No tropical sights for you, Joe, my man. Just tropical air."

"I'll take it," added Elie, who was happy to escape a shaky stomach for a few days. "Let's head up to the deck."

On Friday, the Nouméa port director, Lt. Cdr. John D. Andrews, prepared sailing directions that called for the *Coolidge* to proceed by way of several designated open ocean positions: "Queen," directly north of New Caledonia was the first rendezvous, leading to "Victor," the second-to-last, and ending at "Hypo," before heading to "Button," the final destination. The directions were delivered the next day, and soon a pilot came aboard, and the ship weighed anchor at 1500 hours. She sailed through the submarine net and, about two hours later, said goodbye to the pilot, having passed Amédée Island Lighthouse on the reef and moved into the open sea.[8] Even as they left Nouméa, the men had no official notification of their destination. All they heard was "You'll know when you get there," but it was obvious that the next stop was the New Hebrides. They did not know that they were heading to a great mistake, even though the *US Army Field Manual,* section 100-5, had taught them that "man is the fundamental instrument in war; other instruments may change but he remains relatively constant. Unless his behavior and elemental attributes are understood, gross mistakes will be made in planning operations and troop leading."

9

DISASTER STRIKES

"Anybody know anything about the New Hebrides?" queried a curious Elie late Tuesday evening as the officers sat on their cots.

"I know it's in the western South Pacific, where there are still cannibals on some of the islands."

"Thanks a lot, Charles. We really needed to know that. It looks like we're heading that way."

"I've read a little about that area. What Charles says is really true," confirmed Chuck.

"So have I," Elwood added, "and I think it's true, too; but some of what I learned isn't exactly true. A hundred years ago, the American author Herman Melville went to the Marquesas, and when he came home, he made up stories about his time in the Pacific islands. One of his books is called *Typee*."

"Did you read it?"

"The beginning of it. He described the *Perseverance*, a Nantucket whaling ship of young men that was out in the Pacific for over a year, but its headstrong captain wouldn't let the crew go home until they filled all the barrels with whale oil. After three or four years, her owners gave her up for lost, and even the islands where she was supposed to have touched in had disappeared from the South Sea charts."

"What happened to her?"

"After a long time, she was spotted somewhere near the ends of the earth, casually sailing along with patched-up sails, knotted rigging, and basically in a bad way. Her crew was made up of twenty old salts who hobbled around on deck. Her hull was completely covered with barnacles. Three pet sharks followed them as they went along, looking for scraps from the cook's bucket."

"That's nonsense," scoffed Elie.

"I told you he made up the stories," said Elwood with a smile.

"You know what, Mr. Cook's garbage man? You're full of hot air."

"Yup. But I had you there for a while."

"And what happened to the narrator?" asked Charles, really interested in the clever writer.

"He was captured by cannibals, but in the end, he was rowed out of Typee Bay by a tabooed crew and picked up by the *Julia*."

"No, I mean really — Melville in the Marquesas."

"He and his friend Toby Greene, who had jumped ship there, spent four weeks on the island of Nuku Hiva. They were eventually picked up by an Australian whaler, the *Lucy Ann*, then transferred to the *Charles and Henry* in Tahiti, before signing on to the naval frigate *United States* to get home."

"I hope we get home," mused Chuck.

Similar conversations were taking place below, in the hold. Joe seemed to have abandoned his tomfoolery, as his mates pooled their information about the New Hebrides. Little was added that was helpful. Everyone was excited about reaching dry land, but worried about the possibility of battle.

Joe thought about his conversation with Elwood in Nouméa. He was struggling with his belief. The idea that pain and suffering would be permitted by God was difficult to understand, and it made him wonder what kind of a god God was.

He had only just become aware of the chance that he could die, and he supposed he might need God to get him through, because the situation he was in was so real, so vivid to him. There would be gunfire where he was going. What would happen? He could not stop thinking about it. *If getting to God in Heaven is good and inevitable, then my own death would not be a bad thing — even though everyone says "War is hell."* He was worried about the brutality of war. Would he end up wounded? He conceded that it might be wise to follow Elwood's suggestion to meet with the chaplain, but he was beginning to feel unwell.

On the bridge, Captain Nelson and his officers checked the instructions and plotted their course. Hypo was a point in the archipelago of the New Hebrides, lying due east of Tutuba, an island located at the eastern entrance to the Segond Channel that ran between the islands of Aore and Espiritu Santo. After the Japanese attack on Pearl Harbor, the Allied forces had set up a major military supply and support base on the jungle island of Santo, as the residents called it, because it lay conveniently halfway between Nouméa and the Solomon Islands, and 630 miles southeast of Guadalcanal. The island was code-named Button and later memorialized in *Tales of the South Pacific*. It was to become both a staging point and a rest-and-recuperation destination for thousands of servicemen and -women who lived in Quonset huts — or, more specifically, Pacific huts — not far from its airfields.

The largest and the most northern of the New Hebrides islands, Espiritu Santo, is wooded and mountainous, with rivers and exquisitely beautiful natural pools. It is seventy-five miles long and forty-five miles wide, and its highest peak rises to more than six thousand feet. At that time, under joint British and French control, its ni-Vanuatuan peoples were quiet and peace-loving; and they still are.

In June 1942, a small group of Seabees had arrived with a Marine antiaircraft battery and a company of infantrymen to begin work on an airfield in Turtle Bay. Given twenty days to complete construction, they worked day and night to clear a six-thousand-foot runway that was surfaced with coral. "On July 28, the first fighter squadron [had come] in and was followed the next day by a squadron of B-17's. The planes [had been] fueled from drums and [had given] the Japs in Guadalcanal their first big bombing on July 30."[1] Soon, the Army, the Air Force, and the Marines had arrived. "After the Marines landed on Guadalcanal on August 7, the new field at Santo gave vital support to that action. On August 11, 1942, the 7th Battalion arrived and immediately began construction of more extensive air facilities to support the Guadalcanal campaign."[2] Within two months, another fighter strip was built, and Bomber Fields 1 and 2. The fields were ready and the island was waiting for the five thousand men headed toward it.

The trip was uneventful for the next day or so as Elwood and his men and women sailed to their last point in the Pacific. When the *Coolidge* arrived at Hypo, Merchant Marine captain Nelson was apprehensive, because there was no pilot boat there to lead him through the channel, and he did not want to dally in the open ocean, where the ship would be vulnerable to a Japanese submarine attack.

"Are you going to lie off Hypo and wait for a pilot?" asked Kilton Davis, the first officer. The captain thought it over, weighing the unfamiliar passage ahead of him against the chance of an attack.

"No," he finally decided. "It's too dangerous." There had been nothing in his instructions about mines in the area, and he was not familiar with the demise of the *Tucker*. But he had been very worried about submarine torpedoes, so he proceeded in a direct route toward the Segond Channel.

When Elwood arrived in the soldier's dining room on the morning of October 26 to take charge of the breakfast mess, the sea was calm and the weather warm with not even a breeze. He checked the chow, had a bite to eat, and chatted with the cook staff. The men would be having scrambled eggs and toast, and the coffee smelled wonderful. He thought about Joe, who had gone to sickbay a day and a half ago. Weak and pale, he had given the doctor something to check in his medical books. The doctor was not sure what was wrong. Elwood wondered whether it might be war jitters, but kept that to himself. He had visited Joe the day before, but the patient didn't seem to be getting better.

At 730, the *Coolidge* was spotted by the *USS Sterett* on anti-submarine patrol eight miles ahead, and it made contact. The duty signals officer asked whether it had orders for the *Coolidge*, but the *Sterett*'s response was "negative," so Captain Nelson continued in the most direct route. He did not know that the safe course into the channel required him to turn ninety degrees port at Hypo, before proceeding northward toward the channel.

Shortly, the ship was seen by a patrol craft. *PC479* had relieved the minelayer *Gamble* so that it could return to the harbor to refuel. The *Gamble* was supposed to provide a pilot for ships needing guidance through the minefield at the entrance to the channel. The *PC479*, however, had been given no other instructions than to patrol the entrance, and, at 919 hours, signaling between the two ships was interrupted when the island of Tutuba got in between them. When the patrol craft realized the captain's heading, it gave immediate chase.

The *Coolidge* was now in sight of land, and everything was a mass of green foliage so thick that particular varieties of trees and plants were indistinguishable from the sea. The day was bright and the ocean still calm, so some of the men went on deck to look at Luganville Harbor as the ship moved into the channel. Bill Bradley, senior assistant purser, saw round shapes in the water that he thought were turtles. Second Lieutenant Charles Schubert on B deck knew they were mines.

"My God, there is a mine, and it's going to hit us!" he said.[3] At this moment, a naval shore station began urgently flashing the Morse code message "S-T-O-P," and the *Coolidge* signal man yelled to the bridge "Stop-stop-stop" as the "Stop engines. Full astern" order went to the engine room. The signal man finished out the Morse code: "STOP. You are standing into mines." At 935, in the middle of his words, there was a massive explosion amidships on the port side, and the *Coolidge* lurched; an explosion on the starboard side followed, both near the engine room.

Captain Nelson moved quickly. "Close the watertight doors. Hard right rudder," he ordered, realizing that the best chance to save the men, and as much of the ship as possible, was to beach her on the nearest coral reef. Immediately the klaxon sounded, and the men headed to their "boat stations," just as they had done in the abandon-ship drills.[4] The *Coolidge* started to roll counterclockwise, picked up speed, and headed for the reef. It hit it with a great jolt and both anchors came down. "Abandon ship!" ordered the captain.

10

A Captain's Duty

A fter breakfast, Elwood had stopped in to return *The Song of Bernadette* to Father Mahoney. He had enjoyed reading about the young saint's efforts to be understood and believed, and had appreciated her perseverance, but he hadn't gotten to the end; so he requested to borrow it again after they were ashore. Then he went up on deck.

Balmy breezes greeted him on the bright, sunny morning, and he could hear the seagulls as he looked up at the puffy, white clouds and down at the white-capped waters of the Pacific. He saw coming into view the coastline of a fairly large island of tall, graceful palm trees and scruffy, green piper plants. *This is like a scene from the pictures*, he thought, as the *President Coolidge* glided quietly into a deep channel. He was remembering the cool of October days back home, when the musty brown and orange leaves raked in piles by the curbside heralded baked apples and squash for dinner.

Just then, he glimpsed a low-lying building not too far from a sandy beach. It was right between a pair of slender, leaf-topped trees, and he was sure it was a Quonset hut like those built at home by the Navy's Construction Battalion, the Seabees. He liked the nickname, because it was a pun on CB, and he loved the mental gymnastics of puns.

Back home, he had admired the large billboard of a cartoon sailor bee with a gun and a wrench posted outside the entrance to the Seabees' Quonset Point base in Rhode Island. He thought, *Our men work hard day and night to supply these structures to the war effort, and look where they go: halfway around the world!* In a few yards, he saw some more of the lightweight, semi-cylindrical buildings, most of corrugated steel, but some made of pine to stand up to the wet, muddy conditions of the South Pacific. Elwood was amused to think that he had traveled across the Pacific to see the very same thing that he often saw near the Atlantic.

The appearance of the island of Espiritu Santo prompted him to head down to his stateroom. *Is this just another layover,* he wondered, *or should I begin packing my duds?*

He began to tell Charles about the island. Both of them, aware that the men were eager for a break from the close quarters of the ship, were speculating about whether they would be granted an earnestly desired release or kept on board the way they had been in Nouméa, when —

Wham! There was a forceful blast far below, and they were roughly thrown across the cabin.

"What the —!"

"That was an explosion," yelled Elwood. "Was it the engine, or did we hit something?"

"I think it was a torpedo; we're in dangerous waters," responded Charles with a shaky voice. "Should get to our stations?"

"No. We —"

Wham! There was another blast, this time on the starboard side, their side of the ship, and they were knocked off their feet. Frightened, they gasped for breath, but they knew the drill: they should remain in their stateroom.

If Elwood and Charles were confused and scared, so were the men nearby. They could be heard hollering to each other, trying to determine what had happened. Ed Jaynes tells it this way:

> One of my friends was looking over the side and called for me to come and see this strange object. About then it blew a large hole in the side of the ship. We had caught a line between two mines, so at about the same time the other mine blew. As previously practiced, we returned to our bed area to await the message to evacuate. … Fortunately, the skipper, Captain Nelson, turned toward the beach and the bow hung on the ledge giving us time to get off. In the meantime, the First Mate was screaming "Get off the godamned ship!"[1]

When the klaxon began its awful repetition, Elwood and Charles headed into the C deck passageway, amid a noisy din, and immediately they heard the captain's order: "Abandon ship!" They turned into the lobby just as the ship began to list and found the area packed with men pushing cheek by jowl toward the ladders.

"We can go out this way," called Charles amid the confusion.

"No. I've got to check on my boys and make sure everyone gets out," Elwood shouted back over the racket of the horn, and he headed off in the direction of the mess hall and the galley.

The passageway was beginning to slope, and Elwood had to put his hands on the bulkheads to steady himself as he went. He knew it wasn't far, and, as he forced his way against the tide of men in the narrows, he ran into a sergeant with a group of stewards and cooks.

"I think they're all out, Captain," reported Sergeant Thomas, coming from the galley, where he had been working.

"Did you check the freezers and the bakery? The doors might have slammed shut on them when she hit."

"Nope. Just the mess hall."

"Thanks. Got to make sure," answered Elwood, acknowledging the information, and the sergeant's party elbowed their way toward the ladders.

In two more minutes, Elwood was at the mess. He gave the room, both galley and freezers, a once-over and surprised a couple of recruits still in the bakery, grabbing bread.

"What are you waiting for, men? This is abandon ship." He pushed them out and led them as quickly as possible through the crowd up to B deck, where he supervised their escape in the cargo nets that were being lowered. He knew they could swim to shore through the oily water or get on a raft. He was relieved to note that everyone had on a life jacket.

Elwood was on deck for only a moment when he remembered his buddy Joe. What about the men in sickbay? In the movement of the exodus, had anyone thought about those who might not be able to get out? He turned back into the interior and went down to C deck. The passageways were now slippery, because the toilets and water jugs had slopped over, and, as he navigated through the mess, he almost slid into Father Mahoney.

"Where are you going, Elwood? The other way's out."

"I think Joe Hunt is still in sickbay. Where are *you* going, Father?"

"Well, this morning I was with a man in the brig. I'm afraid he might be locked in."

"Hold on to the rail, Father, and use your hands to pull yourself forward. That way, you won't fall." Both men moved gingerly through the passage a short way and soon parted company.

Sickbay was on the starboard side, but the ship's increasing list made getting there a serious problem. It took Elwood ten minutes to make it, and when he arrived, it wasn't as he expected. He was shocked at what he found: six patients were still there — and only one of them seemed likely to be ambulatory. He went first to Joe, who was barely conscious.

"Joe. Hey, Joe. It's me, Elwood. We've got to get you out of here."

"I'm too sick. Something's wrong with me, Elwood. I can't even sit up."

"We've got to go, right now!" And without any further talk Elwood picked him up off the hospital bed, shifted him onto his back, and hurried out of the room, promising to come back for the others.

Since the angle of the ship was now almost forty-five degrees, speed was important. Elwood knew a barely conscious man could not make it down the cargo nets, so he worked his way toward the C deck first-class doorway. When he got there, he saw above him two officers: his good friend Capt. Warren Covill and Warrant Officer Robert Moshimer. He called to them.

"We've got a sick man here, Warren. Can you lend a hand?"

"Moshimer has a rope. We'll lower it so that you can tie him, and then we'll haul him up." Slowly but surely, with a little help from Joe, the three were able to get him up to the doorway and into the waiting arms of Lt. Ward MacDonald, who had returned to assist.

While they were tending to Joe, Elwood hustled back to sickbay, but his progress was made difficult by the ship's now forty-five-degree list, which caused the passageways to slope so badly that he was partially walking on the bulkhead. When he returned to the foyer with his next patient, the angle had increased even more, and it required great effort for the officers to pull up the invalid soldier.

Back Elwood went for another man: Bill Fusco, the only one who could move adequately with aid. The two of them crawled on hands and knees, arm in arm, through the rising water to the foyer. And Elwood went back again for another, and another, until five had been rescued.

The sixth and last man was the hardest to manage. He was conscious, but could not walk at all, so, totally exhausted and with wobbly legs, Elwood carried him on his back through the passageway, sloshing through knee-deep water. Arriving at the foyer, he used the rope to lash himself to the rail and make it taut between himself and Coville, who had come partway down. If the fellow could pull himself hand over hand just a short way, he could be lifted and pushed upward until he could get to Moshimer, who would hoist him to MacDonald. Elwood held the rope as taut as possible. The men at each station and in the doorway were barely able to hold it in place, and they had to use all their might to drag the fellow over the sill and onto the side of the ship, which was practically flat.

"Let's get you out of there, Warren," Elwood heard Moshimer call down to Coville above him, but the sound was indistinct. He knew his legs were collapsing under him and his eyesight was blurring. Things in his head began to turn. He felt the rope shake as Coville laboriously climbed up and out, to stand next to Moshimer on the nearly level ship. He began to search his pockets for his knife.

"Okay, Euart. It's your turn," he could hear Moshimer call again.

At his words, the *Coolidge* yawed onto her port side, so that the foyer was now completely vertical. Her hull began to rattle and groan.

"Euart, you gotta get out!" Far away now, Moshimer's voice seemed desperately insistent.

No knife. Perhaps it fell out when I was crawling with Fusco. Maybe it's nearby in the water. But he could reach nothing.

"Euart!"

"I'm trying." Elwood whispered. "This knot is as hard as cement!" And his heart began to race, as he worked frantically to untie the knot holding him fast to the rail. There was a deep rumble, and he thought it was like an earthquake. Hearing this, he searched his pockets once again for his knife — trying to think of anything that could break the knot.

"Euart, NOW!" The two officers pulled on the rope in a frenzied effort to bring him up.

"I can't find my knife," Elwood managed to say weakly, as his head spun with the effort. He was completely spent. Exhausted and fading, unable to find his knife or to untie the knot that had been hardened by the man whom he had saved, Elwood prayed.

"My Jesus, save me," he pleaded out loud and began the Act of Contrition that he had practiced as a boy: "O my God, I am heartily sorry for having offended Thee."

At that moment, with a deafening roar, the *President Coolidge* shifted off the coral reef, causing whirlpools to spin uncontrollably and air to burst out in geysers. Nearby "a large self-propelled barge that was attempting to rescue the men went out of control, spinning around and around."[2] Then the ship's stern dropped and began to sink deeply into the channel as her startled prow surged upward in a huge rush of air and dust forced by giant-bubbled spume. With smoke still billowing, her mighty funnels leaned backward, and with a loud gurgling and rumbling, the magnificent ocean liner breached like a great whale, and then sank to the seabed of the Segond Channel.

11

THE AFTERMATH

From boats and water rafts and from the edge of the shore, the soldiers of the 172nd Infantry Regiment and the 103rd Field Artillery
had watched and prayed as the officers on the ship brought men out of
sickbay. From the air above, Pulitzer Prize–winning war correspon-
dent Ira Wolfert, who was flying over the *President Coolidge* at the
time she struck the mines, saw the action below and filed this report,
which was entered into the *Congressional Record* on May 11, 1943:

> The one Army officer [Captain Euart] who died had with-
> drawn to a hold with his men. By the time their turn came to
> leave, the only way out was hand-over-hand on a rope. This
> officer was the last to go, and when he tried, he discovered
> he was too exhausted to pull himself up. He started to call
> for help.

His voice was not a strong one, and there was a lot of noise as the last men aboard were scrambling off. But his life-long friend, Captain Warren K. Covill, United States Army [of East Providence, RI], who had been searching for him and hoping he had got away, heard him and came sliding down to the rescue along with a warrant officer and a defense worker who happened to be on board.

The three men stood on the edge of the hold and tried to haul up the officer who was trapped below by his own exhaustion. The last rescue boat was bobbing up and down alongside the vessel, its occupants shouting to the three men it could see to hurry and warning them there was not a moment to waste. But the three could not bring themselves to abandon the trapped officer.

Then the rescue boat, realizing that it would be dragged down in the last suction of the ship, gave a last despairing warning. The three men did not even turn around.

Captain Covill said he heard all the warnings clearly and that they all heard all the warnings but felt that abandoning their captain was more than they could do.

The rescue boat pulled away hastily with a clanging of the coxswain's bell and a churning and putt-putt of the exhaust. From where I [Ira Wolfert] was I could see the three small, dark figures turn for a moment and watch it go off and then turn back to the hold. Hundreds of men were watching the scene in silence from safe vantage points, and it filled their eyes and filled their hearts to the breaking point.

An extra rope had been found somewhere in the hold and the captain down below there had tied it around his waist and was trying to splice it to the rope held by his would-be rescuers and get pulled up that way when the *Coolidge* went down.

Captain Covill and the two men with him were sucked down with the ship and somewhere down toward the bottom they were thrown to the surface where they could swim to safety.

The captain down in the hold, trapped by his own weariness, died down there.[1]

The soldiers nearby could hear the men calling to Elwood, and when the ship went down, and the last two officers popped up in the water without him, all knew that he had drowned. Walter Wall of Newport, Rhode Island, Elwood's battery commander, still waited hopefully. Everyone was quiet and subdued as they tried to process the loss of their captain and the fear that they had just suffered an attack by the Japanese.

Julius Plato Martin remembers being told to abandon ship by an officer who was white as a sheet because he thought they had been hit by a torpedo. Martin never spoke of these times without getting emotional.

Infantry S.Sgt. Stephen Parisi had also decided on torpedoes. He had felt a "hard right rudder."[2]

But Bill Bradley, senior assistant purser, knew they were not torpedoes, because he had seen the "turtles."[3]

Private Joseph Ignatz of the 172nd reported, "I felt the first concussion, then a second — shortly after. Someone yelled, 'Hard right rudder!' The ship turned towards the shore. It started going down by the stern and tilted to the left. At first no one got off. The ship's crew was preparing for evacuation."[4]

Milt Staley of the 172nd also concluded that it was a torpedo. He was going to take a shower when he saw land and, in his shorts, went to the bow on the port side. He saw a ship and lights flashing in code, and off to right flashing signals. Then they hit the first mine, then the second. He was frightened. When the abandon-ship order came, they were issuing life jackets and the passageways were crowded. The ship was listing to port, and he decided not to get off on that side, because he felt it would turn over on them. He went to starboard and climbed down a rope ladder near the anchor chain. Some men were afraid to jump, so he helped them into boats. He himself swam to shore, cutting his feet on coral. A navy medic bandaged them.[5]

Rhode Islander Edmund C. La Rue of the 43rd Infantry Division got to shore in a boat.[6]

Mortar Sgt. Chester Carpenter of Newport, Vermont, had been assigned to C deck aft, and his company was lined up. A life jacket was thrown to him, and boats were lowered. There were no public-address instructions, but he did not think the ship would sink. The personnel came down on cargo nets to the small boats. Because it was close to shore, there was no panic. He left on the port side aft, stepped into a lighter, and went about one hundred yards to a mine tender. He knew Captain Euart as the mess officer and described him as a smiling "hard worker who took his duty seriously."[7]

As roommates, Elwood and Lt. Charles Stephenson, who later fought in the New Georgia campaign — a part of Operation Cartwheel in the Solomon Islands that was intended to isolate the Japanese base around Rabaul — were told to stay in their cabin after the first explosion:

> They had their bags all packed and their rifles propped up alongside their bunks while they waited for further orders. When one of their rifles slid down to the floor and they began to see the waterline rise up into view out of the porthole, they decided they couldn't wait any longer and had better head up on deck. As they turned to go up the stairs, Captain Euart, who … was a Mess Officer, turned the opposite way and said he was worried about his boys in the kitchen and wanted to go down and make sure none of them had gotten stuck in the refrigerators/freezers which could have swung shut and trapped them.[8]

Second Lt. James Renton heard the klaxon and knew that they had been assigned boat stations. He felt the anchors let go and heard the abandon ship, with everyone in life jackets.[9]

Infantryman Henry Schumacher recalled seeing the palm trees on a warm, sunny, clear October morning. It was breakfast time; there was oil on the water under the escape nets.[10]

Second Lt. Charles H. Schubert, of the 103rd, who slept in a stateroom on B deck, felt the explosion on the port side near the bow, so he checked the staterooms, pushing one door open with his feet. He was the last man to get off starboard aft, but he saw "two fellow officers ... up toward bow ... on B deck ... trying to rescue another officer who had been helping troops." Then the "ship slipped off the reef."[11]

Richard Schneider recounted the following:

On the day of the sinking I was in my bunk. When the ship hit the mine, I fell from the top bunk onto the floor. An alert was given and we were told that the ship was not going to sink. We were instructed to stay in our quarters. Then the ship hit another mine. This time an alert went out that the ship was going to sink and we were instructed to leave. I was on the port side. I made my way to the lobby and remember sitting in a chair. The ship pitched and my chair slid to the other side of the lobby. I made my way to the deck and jumped from the deck to a life boat with three men already on board. We started towards shore and watched the ship go down. ... The ship righted itself up and went down rear end first. It was an amazing sight. I wasn't far from the sinking ship. I could see the water whirling in a big circle as it went down. I lost all of my equipment and personal belongings, escaping with only the clothes on my back.[12]

Max Evans Sr. recalled:

On that fateful day of the sinking, I was on deck and heard people yelling, "Torpedo ... torpedo ... torpedo!" The next thing I knew was that there was an ear-splitting explosion that lifted the front of the ship up. Then when it settled back down into the water, there was yet another explosion. ... It was real hectic about that time. We were led to believe that the ship's captain had panicked and accidentally hit the mines ... troops began stripping there [sic] combat gear preparing to abandon ship.[13]

Roy H. Dobbins, the ship's carpenter, had been in the US Merchant Marines since 1939, and had sailed on the *Coolidge* prior to her having been modified for carrying troops; in all, he had sailed on her for at least thirteen months. He found her to be a beautiful ship. He commented that she burned a barrel of oil per minute for fuel. She sailed quite powerfully. At the time of the explosion, he had just retired from his shift (he couldn't remember the exact time of the day). When the captain blasted the siren, he gathered up only the clothes on his back and his seamen's wallet. He recalls the escape from the ship as a close one. The crew had had lifeboat drills, so he went to his assigned one. He also recalls that "whoever the s-o-b was who was ringing the alarm bells was 'ringing the hell out of the bells.'"[14]

Frank Cameron, who was on board one of the ships in the Segond Channel unloading cargo, described the sinking in an article in *Mast Magazine*:

The first I knew anything was wrong was via the usual alarm of loud excited talk and people running. Silhouetted against the horizon of the channel between Espiritu Santo and Tutuba islands was a large two-funnelled [*sic*] transport. At first I thought it was headed outward until I realized that it hadn't yet been in the harbor and that she was coming at a good speed. By this time I gathered from the talk that she had been hit by mines. Someone said twice, and someone else said three times.

I hadn't heard the explosions but she was listing even then quite noticeably. It was perhaps a minute or two after I arrived on the bridge that she turned broadside to us and the channel, and headed directly for the shore of Espiritu Santo island. She still kept a fairly good speed. She hit the beach head on, about a mile up the channel from where we lay. The chart shows forty fathoms there with plenty of coral heads. No one, I think, had any full comprehension of the impending disaster, since it appeared as though she might be far enough up on the shelf to rest safely while her stern might settle somewhat. It was then 9:45 am.[15]

But she did not settle, and Cameron watched her sink:

A huge geyser appeared by her stern bubbling furiously and she seemed to surround herself with a thin film of smoke as if to curtain the final shame of her death throes. More geysers appeared along her side. Her stacks at last touched the water and then with a tragic gracefulness, her bow rose as her stern settled more deeply and she slid off the coral ledge and disappeared from sight.[16]

The SS *President Coolidge* settled in 100 to 240 feet of water at the bottom of the sea.

The troops moved on to Santo, described by Michener as "the big, brutal island southeast of Guadalcanal,"[17] from which he could see the volcanic island of Ambae, which he renamed Bali Ha'i. Many men surrendered their clothes that had become too oily and received replacements from generous Navy troops.

The next day, their commanding officer held a service for Elwood and a Merchant Marine fireman, Robert Reid, who had been killed by the blast in the engine room of the *Coolidge*.

12

NOTIFICATIONS

In his 2015 bestselling book, *The Road to Character*, David Brooks considers the life of World War II general George Marshall in the context of today's culture:

> We live in a society that places great emphasis on personal happiness, defined as not being frustrated in the realization of your wants. But old moral traditions do not die. They waft down the centuries and reinspire new people in new conditions. Marshall lived in the world of airplanes and the nuclear bomb, but in many ways he was formed by the moral traditions of classical Greece and Rome. His moral make-up owed something to Homer, to the classical emphasis on courage and honor.[1]

Elwood Euart was not a great general; he was a captain doing what he saw as his duty, because somewhere in his education, the classical virtue of courage had taken hold. His was a pure, refined, and deep love for his men that was full of respect, with no hint of selfishness. By participating in the military mission of bringing them up from sickbay, he was paying tribute to the unique and unrepeatable person of each man. He knew these men were worth saving.

His sacrifice was appreciated. Gertrude Hunt of Cumberland, Rhode Island, sister of Joe Hunt, explained to a newspaper reporter how grateful her brother was: "My brother prayed every day of his life for Captain Euart. He was always indebted to him for the extended life he got."[2]

Fr. John P. Mahoney, the regimental chaplain, who was himself a hero in the tragedy, wrote a letter to Mr. and Mrs. Euart on February 14, 1943, letting them know that he had witnessed Elwood's heroism:

> As Chaplain of the 172d Inf. I was on the ship with your son when he gave his all that others might live. "Greater love than this hath no man — that he lay down his life for his friends!" This war has produced and will produce many men of heroic courage; but it is my opinion and, I am sure, that of every man on that ship, there will be no greater hero than Captain Euart.
>
> When we were ordered to abandon the ship, your son was on deck and could have easily, and with honor, slid down the ropes to safety. But with that Courage and Love which is more than human, he went below to make certain that his boys were safely getting off the ship. I saw him there myself as I went down to the brig, to make sure that the boys there had been freed, and especially to check on a mental patient whom I had visited a half-hour before.
>
> The ship had listed to one side, and Capt. Euart had tied a rope about himself and fastened it to a railing so that he could rescue many boys who were unable to climb up the slippery, water-filled ship. And he did rescue them — all! Then just as

he had expended nearly all of his strength in saving others and two of his fellow-officers were about to pull him to safety, the ship went down with all three. Somehow the others were shot up to the surface, but Capt. Euart's body is still tied to his post.

He died doing more than his duty. And his heroic sacrifice has instilled in us all a spirit which will help every man in our combat team to carry on for Captain Euart, and for our beloved Country!

His body is still with the ship, but his immortal soul is with God. I am sure that you need not worry about his spiritual safety.

It seems to me that Capt. Euart had a premonition that he was soon going to Heaven. Although I had met him through Father Cullion back in camp, I came to know him very well on the ship. He had charge of the enlisted men's dining-hall, and although it was being used from early morning until night, he managed to have it cleared for forty minutes each afternoon so I could offer Mass. He attended Mass and received Holy Communion every day, including the Feast of Christ the King, the day before his death.

Captain Euart completed his service to his Country, and today he is in God's Heavenly Army. And with what rank he must have been welcomed by Him who set us the example in giving His Life that others might live! Captain Euart followed that example even unto death!

Just a few days before his death, Captain Euart came to my stateroom and asked for something to read. I gave him *The Song of Bernadette*. The very morning that our ship went down — just an hour before it struck the mines — he came again as I was hearing confessions, to return the book. He had not quite finished it, and asked to borrow it again after we were ashore. I am sure that St. Bernadette told him the rest of the story that day in heaven!

I remember very vividly how he asked me for a copy of "A

Soldier's Prayer," which we say after every Mass. It is a little prayer that I have asked every Catholic boy in our regiment to recite every day. Practically every boy has been "adopted" by some little child belonging to the "Children's Crusade of Prayer"; and in return for the child's daily prayer the soldier was to recite this prayer daily. I had a few blanks on my desk for any other men [other than the 172d] who might wish to be "adopted" by the little children. (Nearly every Catholic member of the regiment had filled out such blanks.) Captain Euart desired to be "adopted"; and he happened to be the only man who actually did fill out one of those blanks during the voyage. That is why I say that he seemed to have a premonition of death.[3]

In his choice to assist others, Elwood showed that he had for God a filial, tender, and sincere piety.

Elwood was one of many brave men in the tragedy of the *Coolidge*. The entire regiment conducted itself in an orderly and obedient manner. Their commanding officer, Col. James A. Lewis, in his General Orders No. 1, dated December 22, 1942, addressed to the members of Combat Team 172, pointed to their "coolness which forestalled panic, trust in your leaders, consideration for the safety of others, [and] agility in scrambling down nets and ropes." He described their plight:

> To wait quietly in a dark and crowded cabin until it grew so steep you piled mattresses on the floor to keep your footing; to move out without stampeding when the order finally came to go; to drop from the dangling net into the green water although you may never have been out over your knees before; to wait for the soldier near you who couldn't swim although you knew you both might be engulfed at anytime by whirlpools when the ship rolled over; to lose no time ashore in building with makeshift tools so you might be dependent on nobody — all reveal something soldiers call "what it takes."[4]

The soldiers had comported themselves well in the emergency, and this was noticed by the congressman from Rhode Island. The Honorable Aime J. Forand read into the *Congressional Record* the following commendation:

Mr. Speaker, the American youth of today, true to the tradition so heroically exemplified by our forefathers, are rendering a glorious account of themselves in every part of the world. They are giving unstintingly all that they have, even their lives, that the enemy might be crushed and that the freedom and liberty which we have known in the past may be preserved as a heritage for the generations that are to follow us.

Every day we read of outstanding feats of heroism. No community has a monopoly on patriotism or heroism. The heroes of this war come from all sections of the country. From the big cities, from the towns, and from remote hamlets.

We of the First Congressional District of Rhode Island, and particularly from the City of Pawtucket, are proud, indeed, of our outstanding hero, Capt. Elwood J. Euart, a 28-year-old soldier who, by lashing himself to the low end of a rope, was able to hold it tight enough for his men to climb to safety, even though their ship, the *President Coolidge*, which had struck a mine in the Pacific, was listing badly. He so exhausted himself that when, after getting all his men out, he tried to get out himself he was unable to do so and went down with the ship.[5]

The morning after the sinking, Father Mahoney, who had borrowed the essentials for Mass from a French missionary, offered a Requiem Mass for the repose of Elwood's soul. Many of Elwood's fellow officers and enlisted men attended. And on the month's anniversary of his death, Colonel McCormick and Headquarters Battery attended Mass for him in a body. A monument placed on the shore near the *Coolidge* reads "In memory of Captain Elwood J. Euart, 103 Field Artillery Battalion, USA October 26, 1942."

A telegram from the War Department notified Mr. and Mrs. Euart of their son's death: "The secretary of war desires me to express his deep regret," it read. "Your son Captain Elwood Joseph Euart died October 26 in South Pacific area by drowning." His grave reads simply "lost at sea."

Six years later, on Saturday morning, April 17, 1948, Elwood's mom and dad; his sisters, Rita, Monica, Eleanor, and Ruth; and his brothers, John and Leonard, gathered at the Rhode Island State House in Providence. By order of the governor, the acting adjutant general, Brig. Gen. James A. Murphy, decorated Winnie Euart with the Rhode Island Cross. The room was filled to capacity with relatives, personal friends, military comrades, members of the clergy, representatives of Rhode Island State College, the public schools, the Veterans of Foreign Wars, and the Boy Scouts (Elwood was a Boy Scout for six and a half years). There was a color guard from the Capt. Elwood J. Euart VFW Post No. 602, and the ushers were from the Sea Scout Ship *Elwood Euart* and the Eagle Scouts.

Dr. Harold W. Browning, vice president of Rhode Island State College, speaking on behalf of the school, paid tribute:

It is in the hour of tragedy that the character of man receives its severest test. It is what a man does then that expresses his true worth and tells what he really is. In moments of sudden crisis the primal instincts of all men is self-preservation. Captain Euart loved life, but, in that final hour of strife on the ill-fated *President Coolidge*, neither the repeated warnings nor insistent urging of his friends, nor his love of life, did he permit to over-shadow his love for his fellow man. Many a man lives today because a devoted islander, with gallant heart, directed and physically assisted his men to safety.[6]

Generations of Euarts and Caseys would grow up hearing the story of Elwood's heroism, recognizing, by their loss, that his self-givenness was a gift that he and his family had made to those he had saved, to the state of which he was proud and its National Guard, and to his beloved country.

13

OFFICIAL INQUIRIES AND OTHER TRAGEDIES

The loss of the *Coolidge* was a serious blow to the Allied war effort in the South Pacific. In his carefully researched book, *The Lady and the President*, which recounts the history of the ship, Peter Stone notes that "the monetary loss was in the millions,"[1] not only the loss of a troop ship, but also supplies, replacements, and medicine. A study of the war logistics lists the "strangling [of] the flow of maintenance supplies and backlogged equipment,"[2] including guns, anti-tank guns, ammunition, gas masks, Jeeps, trucks, and 155-millimeter howitzers; the missing troop replacements for Marines on Guadalcanal; and the disappearance of scarce stores of medicine, specifically 591 pounds of quinine, which at that time was the entire stock held by the United States.[3]

Probably the most difficult consequence, however, was the handling of the incident and its inquiries. Several reports have indicated that the sailing orders for the approach to Espiritu Santo did not include details about how to avoid the American minefields set up to protect the island, which, as the home of the Pacific Naval Command, was planned to be a significant staging point for troops in the South Pacific. (Half a million United States servicemen and -women would be stationed at Santo during World War II.)

Perhaps because of embarrassment or because the location was sensitive, the United States Navy withheld public information about the sinking, until it was pressed to admit in mid-December that "someone had blundered."[4] In fact, between December 1941 and March 1943, there were only four official Navy communiques concerning Espiritu Santo, and none of them mentioned the *Coolidge*.[5] The Merchant Marine master of the *Coolidge*, Henry Nelson, sixty-three, who had saved the lives of five thousand men by running the ship aground to avoid sinking in deeper water, was brought before three official courts.

The first preliminary court of inquiry was convened at the request of Adm. William F. "Bull" Halsey, commander, South Pacific Area and South Pacific Force, on November 12, 1942, aboard the destroyer tender *USS Whitney*. In spite of Captain Nelson's "impeccable record,"[6] and with every officer's testimony that "he had no criticism of the conduct of the master,"[7] and the volunteered information of a few officers "that they would be glad to serve under Captain Nelson again or on another voyage," the court recommended that charges be laid against the master "through negligence suffering a vessel of the United States to be lost."[8]

The matter was referred to a military commission that met at College La Perouse on Nouméa, New Caledonia, on December 8, and was conducted by Rear Adm. Calvin H. Cobb, United States Navy. Questioning centered on "Special Information" that ought to have been attached to a packet of instructions for Captain Nelson from the Nouméa Port Director's Office. Nelson testified that he had never received the information. The commission acquitted him of guilt, and the questioning revealed the startling news that Merchant Marine vessels were not given all available tactical information, especially the location of friendly mines, knowledge that would have prevented the *Coolidge* disaster.

The result did not please the Navy Department, and the captain was referred to an "A" Marine Investigation Board of the United States Coast Guard upon his return to the United States on February 6, 1943. The board, under the direction of Coast Guard Marine Inspection officer Lt. Cdr. Henry V. Barbieri, let stand the Military Commission's acquittal, but it did not exonerate Captain Nelson, as it should have. This may not have been surprising, considering that, by then, the Coast Guard had been made part of the United States Navy. A statement issued in 1963 — twenty years after the investigation — did, however, admit that "the specific locations of our own mine fields were highly classified and never positively identified to individual commanding officers."[9]

In a *San Francisco Call-Bulletin* article of January 29, 1943, Captain Nelson made abundantly clear what had happened: "No information was given to us and no challenge was made by either of the two ships. Just as we entered the real harbor, a blinker message broadcast the one word Stop! But it was too late. Before we could get our engines going full astern, we struck a mine and then another one."[10]

That Captain Nelson ought to have been honored as a hero instead of made a scapegoat seems clear. He certainly was admired as a man of character by his crew, which is apparent in the statement that Roy Dobbins, the ship's carpenter, gave to his daughter:

> Dad stated that he was helmsman in the lifeboat of more than 25 Merchant Marines and U.S. Army soldiers. His lifeboat had reached land when the *Coolidge* sank. He remembers being very sad — as though he had lost a good friend. His admiration for the Captain was maintained as he continued to sail with him on later voyages. Dad continues to defend the innocence of Captain Henry Nelson regarding his situation with the loss of the *Coolidge*.[11]

A salvage recovery was briefly attempted, before the last of the American troops left the island of Espiritu Santo in 1945. Col. Arthur G. King, M.D., chief of the Medical Unit and surgeon of the Espiritu Santo Service Command, was interested in the quinine. On January 14, 1943, he was to make a dive with Navy professionals to rescue what they could find, but one of the mines broke loose that day, the salvage event was canceled, and later no quinine was found. A few local forays into the ship were attempted, but the United States took no interest in her.[12]

On May 8, 1953, Burton Kent Jaquith purchased the *Coolidge* from the United States Department of Commerce for ten dollars, intending to have a Japanese firm conduct salvage, but the New Hebridean government refused to give a permit, and so she lay on the bottom for the next sixteen years. In 1969, a team led by Australian divers Barry May and Des Woodley, along with Allan Power, successfully removed her two huge brass propellers and other metals, and later May recovered field-gun shells, rifle cases, spare wheels, tires, and 105-millimeter cartridge cases. Americans had taken off trucks, Jeeps, and general campaign equipment; and, from 1974 to 1977, at a cost of $92,000, Ian Lockley recovered six hundred tons of bunker C-grade oil, which had become a hazard.[13]

The Vanuatu government declared the *President Coolidge* a protected National Park site on November 18, 1983, and nothing can be taken from her. Since then, she has become one of the most popular diving venues in the world. The *London Times* rated her in the top-ten wreck diving sites in 2007. Thousands of divers have come from all over the world to explore her. She is easy to find, and the sea around her is usually calm and suitable for diving, but it is important to enlist the services of an experienced guide.

Since her sinking, there have been three other tragedies associated with the *President Coolidge*. On November 5, 1980, a Swiss diver on the *Barracuda* who had been diving only with his eight-year-old son, died of a brain hemorrhage after reaching 160 feet, surfacing, and returning to 160 feet.

In November 1996, an Australian master instructor and a Welsh rescue diver became lost after stirring up the silt in the engine room. In her account of this second event in "Legends of the Deep," Jane Hutchinson describes the accident, which had happened two weeks before her own dive:

> [They] had refused to dive with a guide who knew the wreck well and had become lost and trapped in the ship's engine room. It appears one of the pair had panicked, stirring up a blinding cloud of silt from the floor of the wreck that prevented them finding their way out. The rescue team found scratch marks on the metal roof where one of the men had tried to claw his way out. His body was found nearby, his fingers bloodied from the struggle. The other was found some distance away, just a few metres from an exit that would have led him to safety.[14]

As a novice diver, Hutchinson was understandably nervous after learning of the casualties.

A distressingly unnecessary death was that of an American, Dr. Lailande (Osunsade) Healy, on May 2, 2013. After having been unsuccessful in her morning attempt to reach the icon known as "the Lady," a painted ceramic casting of a lady and a unicorn located in the dining room, she and her guide tried again in the afternoon. They swam from the bow of the ship about a hundred meters along the starboard side of the hull and entered through Euart's Door, which, as the primary access for passengers, leads to the main lobby. They descended inside the door to the bottom of the lobby area, into the dining room, and over to "the Lady" on the back wall. After leaving the dining room, Laila, as she was known, dropped eight meters and died on the lobby floor at 41 meters (140 feet) from the surface.

Michael McFadyen, who has dived the *Coolidge* one hundred times or more and maintains a scuba diving website, has chronicled the events surrounding Healy's fatality, including the version of her guide, the profile from her dive computer, events of the recovery, the New Zealand police investigation, and the coroner's findings. His early theory focused on the consumption of air:

> The only real alternative to what happened ... is that Laila
> never actually exited the wreck. This actually has a lot of cre-
> dence, as based on the amount of air she used on the dive
> (120 bar), I cannot reconcile this with the dive as stated. For
> example, if she used air at the same rate that she used it on
> the dive of the wreck on 30 April 2013 (31 liters per minute if
> she started with 220 bar), then she would have used 172 bar
> leaving 48 bar in her tank. Remember that when the tank was
> found it had 100 bar.[15]

McFadyen aided the New Zealand police by comparing Healy's dive
computer to a computer record of a similar dive that he had made
to "the Lady," and found that the account of the accident given by
her guide was inaccurate and that she had never left the wreck: "The
profile seems to show that Laila ascended to 33 metres and then fell
unconscious. I base this on the fact that the descent from 33 metres to
over 40 metres is absolutely constant and the line straight."[16]

Like the event of the *Coolidge*, the mystery associated with this
death has to do with human error. These three tragedies, that either
had no guide at all, or had imperfect guidance, point to the human in-
ability to control all that happens, including when we will be leaving
this earth. As Shakespeare's Hamlet understood well, "There's a special providence in the fall of a sparrow. If it be now, 'tis not to come; if
it be not to come, it will be now; if it be not now; yet it will come. The
readiness is all. Since no man of aught he leaves knows what is 't to
leave betimes? Let be."[17]

14

ELWOOD FOUND

On June 15, 2012, when Rex Moli brought the remains of Captain Euart to Allan Power, the owner of Santo Dive Tours, he restarted a process that would end in Pawtucket, Rhode Island. Six years after the sinking, in August 1948, a search team from the Army's 604th Quartermaster Graves Registration Company had visited Espiritu Santo to recover personnel from underwater losses. The team was able to locate the civilian Robert Reid, who died in the engine room blast; however, it could not complete its investigation of the *Coolidge* because of "the depths involved," and the next month, Euart's remains were declared nonrecoverable.[1] "It was decided it was too dangerous to get to his body, as the *Coolidge* [had] slipped off the reef and down into the channel."[2] No further official attempts were made.

Moli's discovery sixty-four years later, however, "prompted a series of messages from Espiritu Santo to New Guinea to Australia, and then to U.S. authorities in Hawaii."[3] The Joint Prisoner of War/Missing in Action Accounting Command (JPAC) in Hawaii received the information that the diver who had discovered the remains "hid them deep into the silt to keep them safe,"[4] and registered the find.

In 2014, after the merger of JPAC with the historians in the Defense Prisoner of War/Missing Personnel Office (DPMO) and the scientists in the Life Sciences Equipment Lab (LSEL) to form the Defense POW/MIA Accounting Agency (DPAA), an underwater recovery leader accompanied a Santo Dive Tours diver, who pulled possible human remains out of the silt.

The next year, in late February, the United States Army again deployed a DPAA underwater recovery team from Hawaii to the site. On a bright, clear March 3 day, two divers with communications face helmets and without fins, were guided to the remains deep within the ship by dive master Timothy Richie and Moli's friend Yan.

The recovery process took four days and several nights, and they found additional remains and material evidence. Richie said he was "happy to assist in the relocation of the body and then let them get on with the job." All in all, "some 95 percent of Euart's skeleton was recovered, along with his compass, pen and spare change."[5] The team was fortunate to have recovered the remains just days before Cyclone Pam hit the island on March 13, 2015, and shifted some of the silt.

The next step was to verify the remains. Three of Elwood's nephews were contacted to participate in DNA testing, which identified the captain. Scientists conducted a dental lab study, which matched his records, and an anthropological analysis. And on August 24, 2016, the DPAA announced that Elwood Euart's remains had been identified and would be returning to his family for burial. At the family's request, Elwood would be buried at home rather than in Arlington National Cemetery.

He was transported first to Atlanta and then to Theodore Francis Green Airport in Warwick, Rhode Island, where a military and state police escort accompanied his casket to a funeral home near the Pawtucket border. There, the whole state was invited to attend a viewing and presentation of awards. There was a great crowd of veterans, residents, and state and federal officials, including the governor and the state's congressional delegation.

The casket was draped with the American flag and welcomed home by Pawtucket mayor Donald R. Grebien, who had placed a red, white, and blue memorial wreath on display at Pawtucket City Hall.

Rhode Island National Guard Brig. Gen. Christopher Callahan pointed out that "Euart's heroism — to exit a point of safety and enter a dangerous area to save the lives of others — is something that cannot be taught in any branch of the military, but rather was something learned from parents, family and a community."[6] On behalf of the family, Paul Vallee, a nephew, received the Distinguished Service Cross, the second-highest award for valor in the nation, as well as the Purple Heart. The governor of Rhode Island presented the Rhode Island Cross.

A Mass of Christian Burial was held at St. Maria Goretti church in Pawtucket before the interment at St. Francis Cemetery. At that Mass, which was held with full military honors, Fr. Robert L. Marciano, the celebrant and homilist, echoed the thoughts of General Callahan. In Father Marciano's words:

> It came from the depths of his faith, a Catholic faith that he cherished and nourished and loved, attending Mass every day on that ship, worshipping a God whose only Son mounted the finest pulpit of all time — the cross of Calvary — and bowed his head in death so that he could destroy death forever. … How many times had Capt. Euart, from his youngest days, gazed upon a crucifix in his brief life and thought of that? And that as he lowered himself down, tethered to a rope that day, deep into a sinking ship to save others, how Our Blessed Lord must have smiled to see that so many centuries later, brave souls had heard his message and were ready to follow him so that others might live.[7]

On August 31, 2016, Captain Euart was buried in St. Francis Cemetery alongside his parents, in a plot they had purchased for him, hoping that he would be recovered from the Segond Channel one day. Among the mourners was his childhood friend "Big G," George Costa, who had also fought in World War II. A reporter identified him as "one of Elwood's neighbors while they were kids growing up in Pawtucket" and noted that, although he was in his nineties, he "drove himself to the church and cemetery to attend the services." George told him they had played football together. "I knew him because I lived a block away. The family was great, no doubt about that. ... Today is the greatest day for me in a long time. To see a guy come home that you've known and loved."[8]

15

In Memoriam

There have been tributes to Elwood's heroism over the span of many years and from around the world. Probably the most touching memorial has come spontaneously from various countries and walks of life, because in the last quarter century, open-water divers who have swum to the sunken *President Coolidge* have called the entry to C deck "Euart's Door," indicating their familiarity with and respect for the actions of a man they never knew.

The legend of the American captain, however, began on Espiritu Santo not long after his death. On October 12, 1943, the Army christened Euart Passage, the western entrance to the main channel at Espiritu Santo, and named the island's recreation center after him. The people of the island have also been keeping his memory alive.

A white stone marker on the shore of the Segond Channel at the nearest point to the *Coolidge* is a quiet reminder of the life of this generous man. On significant anniversary years, the town of Luganville assembles on October 26 to pay tribute. After the fiftieth anniversary, Col. Stephen Parisi of the 172nd Infantry, representing all the men of the United States Army who fought in the South Pacific, laid a wreath on the memorial. A most formal gathering commemorating the seventieth anniversary was held in 2012. It began with a very moving sunrise ceremony with prayers, a uniformed guard, the laying of flowers on the water, and a party that featured slides and a flaming entertainment. The hit of the evening dinner was a wonderful cake with a replica of the *Coolidge* above green "water," the words "SS Coolidge, 70th Anniversary," and the years in the corners. It was a very festive event. Then they planned a seventy-fifth-anniversary event, and crews began sprucing things up.

More recently, the Elwood J. Euart Association on Espiritu Santo secured land for a World War II museum to be located in Luganville on the shore of the Sarakata River,[1] and, still in the South Pacific, Camp Euart was named at Mangere Crossing in Auckland, New Zealand.

* * *

At home in the United States, Elwood's local newspaper, the *Providence Journal*, printed an editorial on December 23, 1942. Titled "The Beloved Captain," it expressed the great respect that the people of Rhode Island felt for their native son:

> The account of Captain Elwood Euart's death aboard the sinking transport, *President Coolidge*, is to us one of the most moving to come out of the war. And this is not because of the gripping drama of his friends' vain attempt to save him — a scene of heroism which, as Ira Wolfert has said, filled the hearts and eyes of hundreds of silently watching men to the breaking point; but it is because of the inspiring life story of the young officer whose character found its ultimate and logical expression in this supreme self sacrifice.

Elwood Euart was the good captain, not of story, but of the terrible realities which are testing men's souls. He was trusted, respected, and beloved. The eyes and hearts of hundreds of others of us far removed from the scene have also been filled to the breaking point by the story of his great heroism. May we in life live up to the greatness he showed in death.[2]

The Army showed that same respect by awarding Elwood its Distinguished Cross on April 7, 1943. The distinction read as follows:

Captain Elwood J. Euart, Field Artillery, United States Army for extraordinary heroism in connection with military operations against an armed enemy while serving with the 103d Field Artillery Battalion, 43d Infantry Division, in action against enemy forces on 26 October 1942. Captain Euart lost his life after helping to save a number of other men at the time of the sinking of the U.S. Army Transport PRESIDENT COOLIDGE. Learning of a group of soldiers trapped in the infirmary of the ship, he reentered the sinking ship to assist the trapped men. ...

By lashing himself to the lower end of a rope, he was able to hold it tight enough for the men to climb to safety, even though the ship was listing badly. When he finally attempted to climb the rope himself, it was hanging almost vertically. As he climbed, the ship careened and sank. Captain Euart's intrepid actions, personal bravery and zealous devotion to duty at the cost of his life, exemplify the highest traditions of the military forces of the United States and reflect great credit upon himself, the 43d Infantry Division, and the United States Army.

And many other honors have followed. In Pawtucket, the Elwood J. Euart Veterans of Foreign Wars Post 602 at 55 Overland Avenue was named many years ago. His Boy Scout troop #1 Pawtucket and a Sea

Scout ship were named after him.

The University of Rhode Island (formerly Rhode Island State College) inducted Captain Euart into the ROTC Hall of Fame in 2015, and he is named on a memorial for fallen veterans on Upper College Road.

In 2016, the Narragansett Council of the Boy Scouts of America renamed their camp staff scholarship — awarded annually to an outstanding Eagle Scout and member of the Camp Yawgoog staff — in honor of Captain Euart. Capt. James Cunha, United States Navy, retired chairman of the Yawgoog Alumni Association, said, "Achievements and sacrifices like Captain Euart's set an example for all Eagle Scouts."

What we can surmise from this litany of respect for Captain Euart is an understanding that heroic virtue is not out of fashion. There is still evident a love of the good and an appreciation for the selfless deeds of outstanding men and women.

And what are the markers along the way that helped to form the good person? In Captain Euart's story, there were ordinary and extraordinary gifts, but even the ordinary are extraordinary in the grand scheme of things:

the joy of a loving, faith-filled family
the loyalty of a youthful friend
the consistent moral guidance
the dependence of a special-needs sister
the leadership training of the Boy Scouts of America
the gift of poverty
the dignity of work
the necessity of waiting
the sorrow of a lost love
the mature friendship of fraternity brothers
the horror of a catastrophe
the discipline of the Rhode Island National Guard
the bonding of military buddies
and the model of a holy priest

Fr. Larry Richards, the author of *Be a Man*, described Fr. Emil Kapaun, the heroic priest who ministered to the POWs of the Korean War, as a "Man's Man," one who was a hero, holy and real. The same can be said of Capt. Elwood Euart.

Life in Pawtucket, Rhode Island, in college, and in the military had taught him the important lessons in life. He was known by his fellows to be punctual, diligent, and religious. Because he loved his men, he recognized that he had to do what needed to be done to save them in an emergency. His strong faith, nurtured throughout a lifetime, provided the grace to persist in the face of grave danger, so — even though it is certain that he hoped to survive the disaster — he first had to be sure that others did. His is a story of love, service, and human dignity.

Notes

Chapter 1

1. Quoted in Mike Tanier, "Deflategate, Roaring '20s Style: New England's 1st Controversial NFL Champions," *Bleacher Report*, May 19, 2015, accessed June 8, 2021, http://bleacherreport .com/articles/2468402-deflategate-roaring-20s-style-new -englands-1st-controversial-nfl-champions.

Chapter 3

1. John Hogrogian, "The Steam Roller," *Coffin Corner* 2, no. 3 (1980): 6, Professional Football Researchers Association, accessed June 8, 2021, http://www.profootballresearchers.org/coffin -corner80s/02-03-029.pdf.
2. Ibid., 9–10.
3. "A Recollection of What Our Blessed Father Told Our Sister Claude-Simplicienne, a Religious in Our Monastery at Annecy," appendix I A in *The Spiritual Conferences of Saint Francis de Sales*, trans. Rev. William Ruhl, OSFS (Wilmington, DE: Oblates of St.

Francis de Sales, North American Provinces, 1997), 291, accessed June 8, 2021, https://static1.squarespace
.com/static/57082740746fb9895f9277d8/t
/576841c8f7e0ab978ac22372/1466450376901
/spirconf_appendix1.pdf.

Chapter 5

1. National Oceanic and Atmospheric Administration, "The Great New England Hurricane of 1938," National Weather Service, last modified August 8, 2019, accessed June 8, 2021, https://www.weather.gov/okx/1938HurricaneHome.
2. Senior Class of Rhode Island College, *The 1939 Grist* (1939), 249.
3. James Dodson, "Hurricane of 1938: The Wind That Shook the World," *New England Today*, September 20, 2018, accessed June 8, 2021, https://newengland.com/today/living/new-england-history/hurricane-1938/.
4. Ibid.
5. Ibid.
6. Ibid.
7. Ibid.
8. Aram Goudsouzian, " 'What Do You Do with a Disaster?': Providence and the Hurricane of 1938," *Rhode Island History* 62, no. 2 (Summer 2004): 40, Rhode Island Historical Society, accessed June 8, 2021, https://www.rihs.org/wp-content/uploads/2020/02/2004_Sum.pdf.
9. Ibid.
10. *The War Reports of General Marshall, General Arnold, and Admiral King* (Philadelphia: J. P. Lippincott, 1947), 53.

Chapter 6

1. K. Graham Fuschak, "The 43rd Infantry Division: Unit Cohesion and Neuropsychiatric Casualties" (master's thesis, United States Army Command and General Staff College, 1999), 6.
2. Ibid., 13.
3. Jim Ashton, "Camp Blanding: the War Years," *The 30th Infantry*

Division in World War II, "History: Camp Blanding," Camp Blanding Museum, last modified 2000, http://www.30thinfantry.org /blanding_history.shtml.

4. Fuschak, *The 43rd Infantry Division*, 6.

5. Ibid., 8–9.

6. Ibid., 6.

7. Ibid., 9.

8. Ibid., 17.

9. Department of Defense News Briefing, quoted in "There Are Known Knowns," Wikipedia, last edited May 23, 2021, accessed June 8, 2021, https://en.wikipedia.org/wiki/There_are_known _knowns#cite_note-defense.gov-transcript-1.

CHAPTER 7

1. Peter Stone, *The Lady and the President: The Life and Loss of the S.S. President Coolidge* (Yarram, Australia: Oceans Enterprises, 1997, repr., 2006), 24.

2. Ibid., 263.

3. Ibid., 23.

4. Ibid., 24.

5. Ibid., 88.

CHAPTER 8

1. Ibid.

2. Ibid., 87.

3. Ibid.

4. Ibid., 45.

5. Ibid., 88.

6. Ibid.

7. Ibid., 87.

8. Ibid., 90.

CHAPTER 9

1. *Building the Navy's Bases in World War II: History of the Bureau of Yards and Docks and the Civil Engineer Corps 1940–1946*, vol. 2,

pt. 3 (Washington, DC: Government Printing Office, 1947), 228, Naval History and Heritage Command, accessed June 8, 2021, https://www.history.navy.mil/research/library/online -reading-room/title-list-alphabetically/b/building-the-navys -bases/building-the-navys-bases-vol-2.html.

2. Ibid.

3. Quoted in Stone, *The Lady and the President*, 99.

4. Ibid., 97.

CHAPTER 10

1. Fuschak, *The 43rd Infantry Division*, 25.

2. Matthew Laird Acred, ed., "The SS President Coolidge," Asisbiz, last modified July 2019, accessed June 8, 2021, https://www.asisbiz .com/Vanuatu/SS-President-Coolidge.html.

CHAPTER 11

1. Hon. Aime J. Forand, "He Gave His Life to Save His Men," *Congressional Record*, May 11, 1943, A2318, accessed June 8, 2021, https://www.google.com/books/edition/Congressional_Record /DzDExVqAdJ8C?hl.

2. Stone, *The Lady and the President*, 98.

3. Ibid., 98.

4. Acred, "The SS President Coolidge."

5. Peter Stone, "The Lady and the President," *Oceans Enterprises*, last modified 2019, accessed June 8, 2021, http://www.oceans.com .au/pc.html.

6. Ibid.

7. Ibid.

8. Acred, "The SS President Coolidge," as told by Sue Stephenson.

9. Stone, *The Lady and the President*, 97.

10. Ibid., 95–98.

11. Ibid., 99–101.

12. Acred, "The SS President Coolidge."

13. Ibid.

14. Acred, "The SS President Coolidge," as told by Julie Dobbins.

15. Quoted in Stone, *The Lady and the President*, 109.
16. Quoted in Acred, "The SS President Coolidge."
17. James A. Michener, *The World Is My Home: A Memoir* (New York: Random House, 1992), 8.

CHAPTER 12

1. David Brooks, *The Road to Character* (New York: Random House, 2015), 127.
2. Tom Mooney, "After 74 Years, a Hero's Homecoming," *Providence Journal*, August 30, 2016, A1.
3. Reverend John P. Mahoney, letter to Mr. and Mrs. Elwood F. A. Euart, February 14, 1943.
4. Col. James A. Lewis, General Orders No. 1, December 22, 1942, copy belonging to Pvt. First Class Henry E. Hervieux posted on SS *President Coolidge* site and addressed to the members of Combat Team 172, US Army.
5. Forand, "He Gave His Life."
6. Quoted in Stone, *The Lady and the President*, 282.

CHAPTER 13

1. Ibid., 140.
2. Richard M. Leighton and Robert W. Coakley, *Global Logistics and Strategy: 1940–1943* (Washington, DC: Office of the Chief of Military History, Dept. of the Army, 1955–1968), 395, Hathitrust, https://babel.hathitrust.org/cgi/pt?id=mdp.39015031821427 ;view=1up;seq=431.
3. Dennis Cline, *Skeeter Beaters: Memories of the South Pacific, 1941–1945* (Rogers, MN: DeForest Press, 2002), 191; Stone, *The Lady and the President*, 124.
4. Stone, 114.
5. Ibid., 283.
6. Ibid, 131.
7. Ibid., 130.
8. Ibid., 131.
9. Ibid., 140.

10. Quoted in Stone, *The Lady and the President*, 114.
11. Acred, "The SS President Coolidge."
12. Stone, *The Lady and the President*, 154.
13. Ibid., 153–72.
14. Jane Hutchinson, "Legends of the Deep," *The Age* travel supplement, April 5, 1997, 6.
15. Michael McFadyen, "Death on the SS President Coolidge," Michael McFadyen's Scuba Diving Web Site, accessed June 8, 2021, http://www.michaelmcfadyenscuba.info/viewpage.php?page_id=893.
16. Ibid.
17. William Shakespeare, *Hamlet*, act 5, scene 2, lines 217–222.

CHAPTER 14
1. "Soldier Missing from World War II Accounted for (Euart),"
Defense POW/MIA Accounting Agency news release, August 24, 2016, accessed June 8, 2021, https://www.dpaa.mil/News-Stories/News-Releases/Article/924176/soldier-missing-from-world-war-ii-accounted-for-euart/.
2. Walt Buteau, "Pawtucket Hero Coming Home, 74 Years After Giving His Life to Save Six Mates," WPRI.com 12, July 21, 2016, accessed June 8, 2021, https://www.wpri.com/news/pawtucket-hero-coming-home-74-years-after-giving-his-life-to-save-six-mates/.
3. Ibid.
4. "Soldier Missing from World War II."
5. Ethan Shorey, "A Local War Hero, Elwood Euart Is Finally Home," *Valley Breeze*, August 30, 2016, accessed June 8, 2021, https://www.valleybreeze.com/2016-08-30/pawtucket/local-war-hero-elwood-euart-finally-home#.YMuNdfKSmbg.
6. Jonathan Bissonnette, "A Salute to the Captain," *Pawtucket Times*, August 31, 2016, accessed June 8, 2021, https://www.pressreader.com/usa/pawtucket-times/20160831/281479275846663.
7. Ibid.
8. Rick Snizek, "Lost at Sea, WWII Veteran Finally Comes Home

to R.I.," *Rhode Island Catholic*, September 8, 2016, accessed June 8, 2021, http://www.thericatholic.com/stories/Lost-at-sea-WWII -veteran-finally-comes-home-to-RI,8380.

CHAPTER 15

1. Godwin Ligo, "Association Secures Land Lease for WWII Museum Site," *Vanuato Daily Post*, January 13, 2017, accessed June 8, 2021, http://dailypost.vu/news/association -secures-land-lease-for-wwll-museum-site/article_05550fa3 -9587-5204-8422-c74aae19f2b3.html.

2. "The Beloved Captain," editorial, *Providence Journal*, December 23, 1942.

BIBLIOGRAPHY

Acred, Matthew Laird, ed. "The SS President Coolidge." *Asisbiz*. Accessed June 8, 2021. https://www.asisbiz.com/Vanuatu/SS -President-Coolidge.html.

Ashton, Jim. "Camp Blanding: The War Years," *The 30th Infantry Division in World War II*, "History: Camp Blanding," 2000. http://www.30thinfantry.org/blanding_history.shtml.

Bachrach, Louis Fabian. Email to author, June 6, 2017.

"The Beloved Captain." Editorial. *Providence Journal*, December 23, 1942.

Bissonnette, Jonathan. "A Salute to the Captain." *Pawtucket Times*, August 31, 2016. Accessed June 8, 2021. https://www.pressreader .com/usa/pawtucket-times/20160831/281479275846663.

Brooks, David. *The Road to Character*. New York: Random House, 2015.

Building the Navy's Bases in World War II: History of the Bureau of Yards and Docks and the Civil Engineer Corps 1940–1946. Vol. 2. Washington, DC: Government Printing Office, 1947. Naval

History and Heritage Command. Accessed June 8, 2021. https://
www.history.navy.mil/research/library/online
-reading-room/title-list-alphabetically/b/building-the
-navys-bases/building-the-navys-bases-vol-2.html.

Buteau, Walt. "Pawtucket Hero Coming Home, 74 Years After
Giving His Life to Save Six Mates." WPRI.com 12, July 21, 2016.
Accessed June 8, 2021. https://www.wpri.com/news/pawtucket
-hero-coming-home-74-years-after-giving-his-life-to-save-six
-mates/.

Casey, Anna (Grant). Interview with author, October 3, 1959.

Casey, Charles J. Interview with author, December 19, 2017.

———. Interviews with Maryann (McCaffrey) Knag, February 14–
May 22, 2017.

Casey, Edward. Interview with author, April 28, 2017.

Cline, Dennis. *Skeeter Beaters: Memories of the South Pacific,
1941–1945*. Rogers, MN: DeForest Press, 2002.

Costa, George. Interview with Maryann (McCaffrey) Knag. St.
Maria Goretti Church, Pawtucket, Rhode Island, August 31,
2016.

Department of Defense. "The Beached Transport SS President
Coolidge, October 1942, Espiritu Santo." Illustration.

———. DoD News Briefing, Secretary of Defense Donald H.
Rumsfeld, February 12, 2002. Accessed June 8, 2021. https:
//fas.org/irp/news/2002/02/dod021202.html.

———. *US Army, Field Manual 100-5: Field Service Regulations,
Operations*. Washington, DC: Government Printing Office,
1941. Reprint, Fort Leavenworth, KS: US Army Command and
General Staff College, 1992.

Dodson, James. "Hurricane of 1938: The Wind That Shook the
World." *New England Today*, September 20, 2018. Accessed June
8, 2021. https://newengland.com/today/living/new-england
-history/hurricane-1938/.

Espiritu Santo and Amazing Islands of Vanuatu. "70th Anniversary
of Sinking the SS President Coolidge." Vols. 1–4. YouTube video,
1:06. January 22, 2014. https://www.youtube.com

/watch?v=fzzOLtguUUk.

Fuschak, K. Graham. "The 43rd Infantry Division: Unit Cohesion and Neuropsychiatric Casualties." Master's thesis, United States Army Command and General Staff College, 1999.

George, C.P. "Preparation of a Battalion of Field Artillery for Summer Training Activities." *Field Artillery Journal* 14, no. 3 (May–June 1924): 237–241. Accessed June 8, 2021. https://www.scribd.com/document/109803698/Field-Artillery-Journal-May-1924.

Goudsouzian, Aram. " 'What Do You Do with a Disaster?': Providence and the Hurricane of 1938." *Rhode Island History* 62, no. 2 (Summer 2004): 29–48. Rhode Island Historical Society. Accessed June 8, 2021. https://www.rihs.org/history_journal/rhode-island-history-journal-vol-62-summer-2004/.

Hogrogian, John. "The Steam Roller." *Coffin Corner* 2, no. 3 (1980). Professional Football Researchers Association. Accessed June 8, 2021. http://www.profootballresearchers.com/coffin-corner80s/02-03-029.pdf.

Hutchinson, Jane. "Legends of the Deep." *The Age* travel supplement, April 5, 1997.

"In Search of the Cycledrome." ABC6News, February 23, 2011. Accessed June 8, 2021. https://www.abc6.com/in-search-of-the-cycledrome/.

Leighton, Richard M., and Robert W. Coakley. *Global Logistics and Strategy: 1940–1943.* Washington, DC: Office of the Chief of Military History, Dept. of the Army, 1955–1968. Hathitrust. Accessed June 8, 2021. https://babel.hathitrust.org/cgi/pt?id=mdp.39015031821427;view=1up;seq=431.

Lewis, James A. General Orders No. 1, December 22, 1942. Copy belonging to Pvt. First Class Henry E. Hervieux. Posted on *SS President Coolidge* site.

Ligo, Godwin. "Association Secures Land Lease for WWII Museum Site." *Vanuato Daily Post,* January 13, 2017. Accessed June 8, 2021. http://dailypost.vu/news/association-secures-land-lease-for-wwll-museum-site/article_05550fa3-9587-5204-8422-c74aae19f2b3.html.

Mahoney, Rev. John P. Letter to Mr. and Mrs. Elwood F. A. Euart, February 14, 1943.

McCaffrey, Lucy E. (Casey). Interview with author, April 1, 1949.

McCoy, Roslyn Smith. Interview with author, January 3, 2017.

McFadyen, Michael. "Death on the SS President Coolidge." Michael McFadyen's Scuba Diving Web Site, 2016. Accessed June 8, 2021. http://www.michaelmcfadyenscuba.info/viewpage .php?page_id=893.

Melville, Herman. *Typee: A Peep at Polynesian Life*. New York: Penguin, 1972, reprint 1981.

Michener, James A. *The World Is My Home: A Memoir*. New York: Random House, 1992.

Moli, Rex. Interview with Timothy Richie, January 19, 2017.

Mooney, Tom. "After 74 Years, a Hero's Homecoming." *Providence Journal*, August 30, 2016.

Nahmias, Leah. "Providence's Lost Stadium: The Providence Cyclodrome and the City's Sporting Past." *ArtInRuins*, December 12, 2017. Accessed June 8, 2021. https://artinruins.com/property /cyclodrome/.

National Oceanic and Atmospheric Administration. "The Great New England Hurricane of 1938." National Weather Service, last modified August 8, 2019. Accessed June 8, 2021. https://www .weather.gov/okx/1938HurricaneHome.

Nose, Philip. "News from Scout Scribes." *Boys' Life* (August 1913): 24–25. Google Books. Accessed June 8, 2021. https://books .google.com/books?id=eDfMrleAjWwC&printsec =frontcover#v=onepage&q&f=false.

Pawtucket Senior High School. *The Pawsenhi*, Class of 1930. Flickr. Accessed June 8, 2021. https://www.flickr.com/photos /pawtucketlibrary/26332326613/in/album-72157667981116181/.

Power, Allan. Email to author, December 2, 2016.

———. "Search for Capt. Elwood J. Euart." *SS President Coolidge*. Photograph Album. Allan Power website, March 3, 2015.

Richie, Tim. Email to author, January 19, 2017.

Ruhl, William. "A Recollection of What Our Blessed Father Told

Our Sister Claude-Simplicienne, a Religious in Our Monastery at Annecy," appendix I A in The Spiritual Conferences of Saint Francis de Sales. Wilmington, DE: Oblates of St. Francis de Sales, North American Provinces, 1997. 291, accessed June 8, 2021, https://static1.squarespace.com/static /57082740746fb9895f9277d8/t/576841c8f7e0b978ac22372/ 1466450376901/spirconf_appendix1.pdf.

Senior Class of Rhode Island State College. *The 1939 Grist*. 1939.

Shorey, Ethan. "A Local War Hero, Elwood Euart Is Finally Home." *Valley Breeze*, August 30, 2016. Accessed June 8, 2021. https: //www.valleybreeze.com/2016-08-30/pawtucket/local-war -hero-elwood-euart-finally-home#.YMuNdfKSmbg.

Siever, Lisa (granddaughter of Edmund La Rue, 43rd Infantry Division). *SS President Coolidge* site, December 27, 2016.

Snizek, Rick. "Lost at Sea, WWII Veteran Finally Comes Home to R.I." *Rhode Island Catholic*, September 8, 2016. Accessed June 8, 2021. http://www.thericatholic.com/stories/Lost-at-sea-WWII -veteran-finally-comes-home-to-RI,8380.

"Soldier Missing from World War II Accounted for (Euart)." Defense POW/MIA Accounting Agency news release, August 24, 2016. Accessed June 8. 2021. https://www.dpaa.mil/News -Stories/News-Releases/Article/924176/soldier-missing-from -world-war-ii-accounted-for-euart/.

Stone, Peter. Email to author, December 5, 2016.

———. *The Lady and the President: The Life and Loss of the S.S. President Coolidge*. Yarram, Australia: *Oceans Enterprises*, 1997, reprint, 2006.

———. "The Lady and the President." Oceans Enterprises, last modified 2019. Accessed June 8, 2021. http://www.oceans.com.au /pc.html.

Tanier, Mike. "Deflategate, Roaring '20s Style: New England's 1st Controversial NFL Champions." *Bleacher Report*, last modified 2019. Accessed June 8, 2021. https://bleacherreport .com/articles/2468402-deflategate-roaring-20s-style-new -englands-1st-controversial-nfl-champions.

Trostel, Philip. "Beyond the College Earnings Premium. Way Beyond," *Chronicle of Higher Education*, January 29, 2017. Accessed June 8, 2021. https://www.chronicle.com/article/beyond-the -college-earnings-premium-way-beyond/.

United States Congress. "He Gave His Life to Save His Men." Extension of Remarks of Hon. Aime J. Forand of Rhode Island in the House of Representatives. *Congressional Record*, May 11, 1943.

"United States Army in World War II." In *The War Department, Global Logistics and Strategy 1940–1943*, by Richard M. Leighton and Robert W. Coakley, Washington, DC: Center of Military History, 1955. Internet Archive. Accessed June 8, 2021. https: //archive.org/details/globallogisticss00leig/mode/2up.

ABOUT THE AUTHOR

Sr. Lucia Treanor, FSE, a Franciscan Sister of the Eucharist, is the author of *Symmetrical Patterning in Franciscan Writings of the Late Middle Ages* and several articles about the compositional structure of fiction. A lecturer at the Catholic University of America in Washington, DC, she divides her time between the Franciscan Life Process Center in Lowell, Michigan, where she raises chickens, and the Franciscan Center at St. Philip Church in Falls Church, Virginia. In 2020, she was a visiting professor at the Catholic University of Eastern Africa in Eldoret, Kenya, where she enjoyed teaching students from Tanzania, Uganda, South Sudan, and Kenya.